CIVICS 102

STORIES ABOUT AMERICA'S CITIES

ROGER L. KEMP

author HOUSE

AuthorHouse™
1663 Liberty Drive
Bloomington, IN 47403
www.authorhouse.com
Phone: 833-262-8899

Published by AuthorHouse 11/29/2021

ISBN: 978-1-6655-4614-0 (sc)
ISBN: 978-1-6655-4613-3 (e)

Library of Congress Control Number: 2021924116

Print information available on the last page.

Any people depicted in stock imagery provided by Getty Images are models, and such images are being used for illustrative purposes only.
Certain stock imagery © Getty Images.

This book is printed on acid-free paper.

DEDICATION

This book is dedicated to Kieran,
The best and the brightest

CONTENTS

Acknowledgements...xi

Preface xiii

Lesson1: America's Cities

How Cities Operate and Function...1

The Names of Municipal Governments...2

How Cities Change Over Time...3

Ways to Work for an Education..4

Cities That I Lived and Worked In...5

Job Opportunities and Desired Locations...6

Political Party Affiliations 7

Lesson2: Elected Officials

How Mayors Are Elected...11

How Mayors Are Selected 11

Maintaining A City's Public Infrastructure 12

Job Interview Question – Annual Salary 13

Job Interview Question – Education..14

Job Interview Question – Minorities 14

The Mayor's Letters...15

The Mayor's Question 16

Lunch with the Mayor 17

The Grant Application 17

The Mayor's Parking Tickets..18

Mayor Wanted to See Me 19

Lesson3: Appointed Officials

Preparation for City Manager Job Interview 23

My First City Manager Job 24

Applying for a Job in a Wealthy Community 24

City Manager Job Requirements 25

City Managers and Economic Development..26

Contract Labor Attorney Services...27

The Best Way to Hire Department Managers 27

The Library Director..28

Professional Department Managers 29

Doing the Right Thing...30

Lesson4: Politics of City Governments

The Location of Polling Places 33

City with Large Minority Population 33

Citizen Complaints About Employees 34

Altering an Employee Union Agreement 35

Police Access to a Military Base...36

Police Officer Salary Increases...36

Police Officers and Computers...37

Police Discounts at a Local Restaurant 38

Invited to Speak to Church Leaders...39

The Headquarters of the "Hells Angels" 40

Being Stopped by the Police – Speeding 41

Gifts from Citizens..41

Lesson5: Finance and Budgeting Services

Mayor's Request to Balance the Budget 45

The City Council Finance Committee 45

The City Council Budget Approval Process..46

Balancing a City's Annual Budget 47

Possible Budget Reductions 48

Compare Your City's Property Tax Rate 49

Citizen Budget Request 49

Union Labor Contracts 50

Departmental Programs and User Fees...51

Personal Property Taxes...52

Contracting Out Public Services 52

Funds for the Homeless Shelter 53

City With a Municipal Marina..54

City With a Public Golf Course 55

Lesson6: Police and Fire Services

The Chief of Police Appointment Process...59

The Chief of Police And The Police Commission..59

Charges Against the Chief of Police 60

Our City's Murder Rate 62

Request from the Chief of Police 62

Police Services in a Wealthy City..63

Police Officers and Local Politics 64

Tour of City by Police Officer 65

Police Walking Patrols...66

Walking in Our Downtown 66

A Police Officer Called..67

Being Stopped by the Police – Red Light...67

Fire Fighters and Local Politics...68

Closing a Fire Station 69

Lesson7: Other City Service

Departmental Services Change Over Time 73

Employee Job Interview Questions...73

Citizens Use of Public Property..74

Property Tax Collections...75

Regulating Business Locations 76

Public Hearing Officer..77

Employee Health Benefits Audit 78

Trees on Our Main Street 79

Accommodating the Homeless 80

Processing Citizen Complaints 81

The Imprisonment Process 82

More Minority Police Officers 83

Lesson8: Other City Topics

Citizen Request to Hold Down Property Taxes 87

Citizen Taxation Request 87

Senior Citizens and Property Taxes 88

Avoiding Vehicle Taxes..89

Personal Property Taxes...89

Privatization of Public Services 90

Doing What Is Right – Getting A City Building Permit 91

Speaking to Prisoners at the Prison..92

A Wonderful Meeting at a Conference 93

The Name of a Major University 93

Where the Alamo is Located 94

The Size of Central Park 95

Lesson9: The Future

City Politics Change Over Time 99

Homeland Security and Our Nation's Cities 99

Homeland Security and Our State's Cities.. 101

Centralized City Purchasing... 102

Making Your Shopping Mall Safer 103

The Shopping Mall in Our Towns 104

Immigrants on the West and East Coasts of the United States 105

Downtown Improvements 106

My Books – Past, Present, and Future 107

Work Accomplishments 108

Additional City Resources from Professional Associations and Other Organizations 110

Appendices 113

    A. Glossary of Terms 115

    B. Local Government Historical Document 125

    C. United States Voting Rights History 126

    D. Model City Charter Election Guidelines 129

    E. Model County Charter Election Guidelines 134

    F. National Resource Directory 139

    G. State Municipal League Directory 146

    H. State Library Directory 150

    I. Books by Roger L. Kemp 156

    J. World Travels by Roger L. Kemp 159

    K. Some Final Thoughts 160

ACKNOWLEDGEMENTS

Grateful acknowledgements are made to the elected officials, appointed officials, and citizens, of those cities that I have worked and lived in during my over a quarter-century public service career on both coasts of the United States.

These states and cities include the following:

- In California — The City of Oakland
  The City of Seaside
  The City of Placentia
  The City of Vallejo

- In New Jersey — The City of Clifton

- In Connecticut — The City of Meriden
  The Town of Berlin

While I served as a full-time City Manager, I taught public administration course in graduate programs at universities located close to where I worked as a City Manager. In one or more cases, the school was a distance away, but the courses taught were on-line.

The universities include the following:

- In California — California State University, Fullerton
  California State University, Long Beach
  Golden Gate University, San Francisco
  University of California, Irvine

- In New Jersey — Fairleigh Dickinson University
  Rutgers University

- In Connecticut — Central Connecticut State University
  Charter Oak State College
  Southern Connecticut State University
  University of Connecticut
  University of New Haven

- In Minnesota — Capella University

PREFACE

Citizens generally have a desire to learn more about America's cities, including their own community's municipal government. This is true because people spend most of their lives living, working, and paying municipal taxes in cities. Many citizens, however, know more about their state and federal government, than they do about the city in which they live. This is primarily due to the extensive media coverage given to topical issues and news events, plus what they, as students, were never taught in high school civics classes many years ago.

City government is the level of government of which citizens should be most informed. After all, the decisions made by local elected public officials – mayors and city council members – have a more direct and greater impact on their lives than do those decisions made by elected leaders in higher levels of government. This thirst for knowledge is made apparent when speaking before community groups and professional organizations about how municipal government works. Most citizens want to know more about the operations of their local government, including the roles of their elected officials, advisory bodies, chief administrative officer, and the various functional managers that make government work.

It is a shame that most high school civics classes, while starting the semester with aggressive goals to educate students about all levels of government, end before reaching the level of government closest to the people – municipal government. The author remembers how quickly the semester ended, usually right after learning about two of the three levels of government. But typically, never covering cities and, if so, only briefly providing a nominal understanding at best. In the field of higher education, this topic is generally thought to be too elementary to be included in college-level classes. Hence, this work has been titled *Civics 102*.

For these reasons, the author has written a collection of stories based on a quarter-century of actual experience working in various communities, and his relationships with their elected officials and citizens. This experience was gained in politically, economically, and racially diversity communities on both the East and West Coasts over an entire life of public service. During his career, the author has served a dozen mayors, several city councils, and scores of local elected officials.

This collection of stories comes from the author's over 25-years of experience serving as an appointed municipal chief executive officer in cities located on both coasts of our nation. To provide insights into the various facets of America's cities, this volume has been divided into nine sections, or lessons. Each lesson should provide the reader with an understanding and insight about particular important aspects of our cities. Together, they will provide the reader with a better understanding about our nation's cities, their politics, as well as how they function, operate, and provide public services to their citizens

Lesson One, *America's Cities*, examines how cities operate and function, the names of municipal governments, and how cities change over time. Options for citizens to work to achieve an education are also discussed. Also, cities that the author has lived and worked in are examined, as are how to pick desired locations to live and work in, and appropriate political affiliations for local government professionals.

Lesson Two, *Elected Officials*, examines how mayors are elected and selected. The role of elected officials in maintaining a city's public infrastructure is also reviewed. Several typical interview questions for city manager job applications are also reviewed. Some examples of real-life experience of a city manager dealing with a city's elected officials are examined. An example of how a city manager should look for a new job is also explained.

Lesson Three, *Appointed Officials*, examines how an applicant should prepare for a city manager job interview, and answer questions from elected officials during the job interview process. A detailed listing of city manager job requirements is also examined. How other departments managers are selected and appointed and the best department manager selection process used by the author, are discussed in detail. How to do the right thing during the selection process is also discussed.

Lesson Four, *Polities of City Governments*, examines where polling places should be located in a community, how to deal with citizens in a large minority community, was well as how to handle complaints from citizens about city employees. Other examples are reviewed that include dealing with elected officials, public employees unions, and related employee issues, as well as how cities deal with higher levels of government, like a military base operated by the federal government.

Lesson Five, *Finance and Budgeting Services*, reviews several important issues relating to dealing with and managing a city's budgeting process, as well as how to properly manage a city's finances. How a city manager should respond to inquiries made by elected officials on how to balance a city's budget are also examined. How to properly balance an annual budget is also reviewed, as are the best possible budget reductions to make, if you have to make them. Other important topics, like contracting out public services, comparing city property tax rates, and working with the employee unions to balance a city's budget, are also examined.

Lesson Six, *Police and Fire Services*, examines the Chief of Police appointment processes, how a city manager should deal with alleged charges against a Chief of Police, and related police and fire issues. Some examples are given on how police services are modified to fit a community's law enforcement needs. Including downtown walking and bicycle patrols. How a city manager should relate to police officers individually is also examined. The role of fire fighters and local politics, and the politics of closing a fire station, are also discussed.

Lesson Seven, *Other City Services,* examines how a city's departmental services change over time, as well as the type of questions asked to job applicates for city positions, which also have changed over time. The use of public property by citizens, property tax collection rates, regulating business locations, and how to do a health benefits audit, are reviewed in detail. Other topics include the role of a public hearing officer, dealing with merchants on downtown improvements, and what cities do to accommodate their homeless population. Dealing with sensitive citizen complaints is also examined.

Lesson Eight, *Other City Topics*, how to properly deal with citizen complaints, how some citizens avoid some of their taxes, how cities deal with senior citizens and their property taxes, are examined. The rules that a city must follow if they wish to contract out any of their public services are also examined. Other personal experience of the author, a career city manager, are also reviewed in detail. Some details about selected cities are also examined. Other topics that did not fit into the other Lesson sections of this book are examined in this section.

Lesson Nine, *The Future*, examines how city politics change over time, and how our nation's cities, and their respective states, are dealing with homeland security issues. The advantages of centralizing the purchasing function is also examined. How cities can make their shopping malls safer is discussed. The changing nature of shopping malls is also examined. Details of the author's books are included for reference purposes. Details of the advantages of working in a city government are explained. Additional internet resources are listed for the reader's reference if they wish additional information in any of the fields related to city governments.

The appendices section of this book contains eleven (11) entries directly related to the Lessons and subjects contained in this volume about America's cities. These documents are explained in simple terms below, so the reader can reference the information resources that are continued in this section, if they wish to do so. An explanation of these appendices are highlighted below.

- Appendix A is a glossary of common terms related to our levels of government.
- Appendix B the document adopted by Mecklenburg County in 1775 to declare its independence from Great Britain.
- Appendix C is a history of United States voting rights laws, starting in 1776.
- Appendix D shows national guidelines for the election processes held in our city governments.
- Appendix E shows national guidelines for the election processes held in our county governments.
- Appendix F is a national resource directory of city resources provided by non-profit organizations.
- Appendix G is a national directory of Stat Municipal Leagues, by state.
- Appendix H is a national directory of Stat Libraries, by state.
- Appendix I is a listing of books published by the author as author/editor.
- Appendix J is a listing of world travels by the author during his public service career.
- Appendix K reflects some thoughts about America's cities for the reader to enjoy.

These stories are a reflection of the experience gained and the battle scars received from over two decades of service as a city manager. This work should provide insight to citizens wishing to learn more about the workings of America's cities, or merely the operations of their own community's municipal government. Lastly, this volume will enhance the reader's understanding about cities in general – the place where they live and spend most of their lives.

The author hopes that readers enjoy these stories as much as he enjoyed writing them and preparing this volume. Without further ado, it's now time to turn to Lesson One! While there is no final examination at the end of these lessons, it is hoped that, after reading this book, citizens will become more astute in their deals with the public officials and bureaucrats at City Hall who run their community's government.

Roger L. Kemp

LESSON ONE

AMERICA'S CITIES

How Cities Operate and Function

Different forms of local governments are managed differently, depending upon the type of government they are. While they are managed differently, they all have Commissions and Boards, that are created by a city's elected officials and/or their voters when they approved the Charter that formed and created their city. For the most part, each City has the same type of departments, since they primarily perform the same services to their citizens.

In the strong-mayor form of government, the mayor is the elected Chief Executive Officer, who appoints and removes department managers, and manages the daily operations of the city. In the mayor-council form of government, the mayor works with the city council, who must approve his major decisions, like hiring and firing department managers. In the Council-Manager form of government, the City Manager hires and fires all department managers, and manages the daily operations of the city that he/she was hired to manage.

From a Board and Commission standpoint, the major Boards and Commissions in a community consists of the following, which may vary slightly from City to City.

- Conservation Commission,
- Economic Development Commission,
- Ethics Board
- Library Board,
- Parks and Recreation Commission,
- Planning Commission,
- Public Safety Commission,
- Public Utilities Commission,
- Retirement Board,
- Senior Citizens Commission,
- Zoning Board of Appeals, and a
- Zoning Commission.

Some cities may be different, from a functional standpoint, and may have additional Boards and Commissions, such as the following ones:

- Golf Course Commission,
- Historic District Commission,
- Harbor Management Commission,
- Public Parking Commission, and a
- Wetlands Commission.

From a functional standpoint, the major departments of a typical city are highlighted below. In the Council-Manager Form of Government, the mayor and city council always appoint two people, the City Attorney and the City Manager, and the City Manager appoints all other department managers. The major departments of a typical city are highlighted below:

- Building Department,
- City Attorney,
- City Clerk,
- City Manager,
- Finance Department,
- Fire Department,
- Human Resources Management Department,
- Information Technology Department,
- Library Department
- Parks and Recreation Department,
- Planning Department,
- Police Department, and the
- Public Works Department.

In some states, County governments do some work for the cities within their respective boundaries, like property assessment services, property tax collection services, and health services. They provide these services to the citizens in their respective cities, and bill these cities accordingly for the work they perform for them.

The formation of some departments may vary, depending upon the size of a city. For example, in a medium sized city, the Economic Development function may be in the Office of the City Manager, or it may be a function assigned to the planning department. In a larger community, they may have an Economic Development Department.

While there are some variations in a city's Boards and Commissions, and their Departments, their Boards and Commissions may be added and modified by a city's elected officials, their mayor and city council members, and maybe by their City Manager, with the approval by a city's elected officials.

Also, since the mayor is a city's highest elected official, and he/she spends time at city hall, a city typically has an Office of the mayor. Usually, the city council shares an office and it is called the Office of the city council, which is located close to the Office of the mayor, and they usually share a secretary too.

If a citizen wishes to find out more information about their city, almost every city in America now has an online website, where most of this information is shown and described. A subject menu for each category is usually listed at the top of each city's respective website.

The Names of Municipal Governments

The names of municipal Governments is determined by the State Government that they are located in. This is how local governments are named in the States throughout America.

When I lived in the State of California, municipal government were all called cities. California also had county governments for their local unincorporated areas.], that had not yet been incorporated as cities. When I lived in California I lived in a city and also in an unincorporated area. Later the citizens in the unincorporated area that I lived in voted to incorporate it, and they approved the name of their city in this process.

When I lived in the State of New Jersey, all local governments were called cities and towns. Usually when they were named by their State Legislator, the small municipalities are called towns, and the larger municipalities are called cities. New Jersey also had county governments, but they all included incorporated cities within their respective county government boundaries.

Then, when I lived in New England, in the State of Connecticut, they only had cities and towns, and this definition was approved decades ago. Small municipalities were called towns, and large municipalities were called cities. Connecticut originally had County Governments too, but the State Government eliminated them in the early 1960's as an economy measure. There are no more County Governments in the State of Connecticut.

Only two states in our nation, have no county governments—one is Rhode Island, that never did, and the other is Connecticut, because their State Legislator eliminated them many years ago.

So, in other states throughout our nation, there are other names for their municipal governments, and some of them include, outside of cities and towns, boroughs, townships, parishes, and villages.

Since many citizens only live in one state, they only know the names of the municipalities in their respective states.

If you wind up working in municipal governments, like I did, you know what I have learned over the years, that each State names their own local governments, and that they are called whatever their respective State Legislatures called them when they were named.

I encourage our citizens, when they move to another State in the future, to check on their respective State Government's website, to see what their State calls their respective municipal governments.

How Cities Change Over Time

In one city that I was the City Manager of for several years, I noticed how its population had changed over the years. I learned this from looking around, and from talking to city employees and citizens, who had lived and worked in the city over the years.

In the olden days, the downtown area was occupied by immigrants from European countries, like France, Germany, Ireland, Italy, and Poland.

The citizens that immigrated to our city, and lived in our downtown area, included people that were French, German, Irish, Italian, Polish, and other European Countries.

Our downtown area had, in the olden days:

- French restaurants and cafes,
- German restaurants and cafes,
- Irish restaurants and cafes,
- Italian restaurants and cafes, and
- Polish restaurants and cafes.

Nowadays, the downtown area in this city has:

- Two Brazilian restaurants,
- A Caribbean grocery store,
- Several Mexican restaurants,
- A Jamaican restaurant,
- Some Latino tax and legal services offices,
- Several Latino barber shops and beauty salons,
- A Puerto Rican café and bar, and
- Other businesses stated by immigrants from Mexico, Central America, and South America.

The city's downtown area had changed greatly over the years. The original immigrant population, as the years went by, either relocated, moved in with their children as they aged in another city or state, or passed away because of old age.

Cities change over time, basically because of the different types of people that relocate to ad live in them over the years!

On the East Coast this includes citizens that relocated to America from countries in Europe over the years, and on the West Coast it includes citizens that relocated to America from Asia over the years.

After all, America is "The Land of Opportunity" and citizens from all over the world have relocated to it over the years. In many cases the children of the families that relocated to America have become more successful than they would have been in the country of their origin

Ways to Work for an Education

After high school, I joined the military service, the U.S. Coast Guard, and once I received a permanent assignment it was in the District Office, of the Coast Guard District located in Southern California, and I lived in the City of Long Beach for three-plus years.

Since I had a nine-to-five job, my evenings were free, and it did not take too long before I enrolled in Long Beach City College, and went to night school at their Liberal Arts Campus for three-plus years and received an A.A. Degree before I got out of the military service.

When I left the U.S. Coast Guard, I returned home to the City of San Diego, got a full-time job and went to night school at Fowler College of Business, at Diego State University. It took me two years to receive a B.S. Degree in Business Administration, with a minor in Psychology, while working full-time.

I went on to graduate school at San Diego State University, in their School of Urban Affairs, and received an M.P.A. Degree in Public Administration. It took me two more years to get this degree, since I continued to work full-time and go to school at night.

I had time left on the F.I. Bill, and thought that I should receive a doctoral degree in public administration. Since I had to work full-time and had to go to night school, I checked throughout the State of California, and only two universities had evening doctoral degree programs in the field of public administration. One was in the City of Los Angeles, and the other was in the City of San Francisco.

I applied for the doctoral program at the Golden Gate University, in San Francisco, was accepted, and got a full-time job in the City of Oakland. I went to night school, while working full-time in the office of Budget and Management Services, then in the Office of the City Manager, before I received my Ph.D. Degree in Public administration, from the Graduate School of Urban and Public Affairs, at Golden Gate University. The same month that I received this degree, I was appointed as City Manager.

During my city management career, I attended two specialized educational programs, where each of the cities that I worked for sponsored me, paid my way, and each of these programs improved my general management and financial management skills where I worked.

One program was the Program for Senior Executives in State and Local Government, at the John F. Kennedy School of Government, at Harvard University. This was a three-week program that let me meet other public executives in state and local governments from throughout our nation, and taught me the best practices in this field. The city that I worked for benefitted from this!

Most people that attend college, go to a local school near where they live. My educational experience was a good example of this. I went to a city college when I was in the U.S. Coast Guard since I lived in this city. I attended public universities when I lived in San Diego, and then went to a private university for a doctoral degree when I lived in the City of Oakland.

Most citizens go to college not far from where they live, and I am a good example of this. Since I had to work full-time, I went to public colleges and universities to work for undergraduate and graduate degrees. When I wanted to pursue a doctoral degree in my field, I got a job in a city close by to the school that offered this program, and it was only offered at a private university, that was not located far from where I lived. It took me five years to complete this program. I received a City Manager job soon after this.

Later during my city management career, the two advanced educational programs that I went to at Harvard University and the University of Wisconsin, the cities that I worked for sponsored me, paid my way, and benefitted from my training in both of these programs, since I continued to be employed by them during the coming years.

Other citizens are encouraged to follow this trend. Working full-time and going to school in the evening. And getting your employer to sponsor you and pay your way to attend other professional executive programs, since your employer greatly benefits from them!

▌Cities That I Lived and Worked In

I was born in the City of Saint Paul, Minnesota, the capital city of the State of Minnesota. It has a population of about 309,000, and was incorporated in 1854. When I was just a child, my parents packed up our things, and my dad drove us to the State of California, since it was "The Land of Opportunity."

We arrived in Hollywood, a neighborhood in the City of Los Angeles, California. The City of Los Angeles has a population of about 463,000, and was incorporated in 1850. I went to grade school in Hollywood, and several years later my family moved to the San Diego area.

We relocated about 20 miles east of the City of San Diego in an unincorporated area called Santee, and it was a rural community that was not yet a city. I lived there through my younger years. Santee was later formed into the City of Santee, which has a population of about 58,000, and was incorporated in 1980.

After high school, I joined the United States Coast Guard, and for nearly four years I lived in the City of Long Beach, south of Los Angeles, and located in the Los Angeles Metropolitan Area. This city has a population of 463,000, and was incorporated in 1897.

When I got out of the military service, I attended school on the G.I. Bill, and received an AA, BS, MPA, MBA, and PhD degrees at public and private universities. After this I started my public service career, and lived and worked in the following cities during my city management career. The number of years that I worked in these cities is also noted below.

City	State	Population	Incorporated	Dates	Years of Service
Oakland	California	433,000	1852	1974-1979	5
Seaside	California	34,000	1954	1979-1983	3
Placentia	California	51,000	1926	1983-1987	4
Clifton	New Jersey	85,000	1917	1987-1993	7
Meriden	Connecticut	60,000	1906	1993-2005	12
Vallejo	California	122,000	1868	2005-2006	2
Berlin	Connecticut	21,000	1785	2006-2008	2

During my public service career, I served in seven cities, that were located in three states on both coasts of the United States, with populations ranging from 21,000 to 433,000, most of them were long-standing cities. I served in them for about 34 years, with an average city manager tenure of almost 5 years in each of these cities.

I liked to work in our nation's cities, and enjoyed restoring their Main Streets, holding down their citizens taxes, and promptly responding to all citizen inquires – regardless of a persons age, gender, race, social, or economic tatus, wherever they lived in the city that I served in as their City Manager.

Job Opportunities and Desired Locations

When I was a City Manager in Southern California since it was the only state that I ever lived in at the time, I always enjoyed my trips to the East Coast, when I went to cities like Boston to attend professional conferences, and New York City when I went to Wall Street to assist in my city's bond ratings.

I went back to Boston and New York whenever possible, since I enjoyed these two major cities in our Northeast and had never visited them before I became a City Manager.

Also, the more that I went "Back East" the more I like the Northeast and New England areas of America.

People would ask me sometime what the difference was between the Northeast and New England. I would respond to them by saying that New England included six states, as follows:

- Connecticut,
- Maine,
- Massachusetts,
- New Hampshire,
- Rhode Island, and
- Vermont.

And the geography of the North East includes two additional states, and they are:

- New Jersey, and
- New York.

After a while, I definitely liked the Northeast, as well as the New England area, since they had seasons, and many trees had their leaves that changed colors during the four seasons during the year.

One time, when in Southern California, I saw a job opening in New Jersey, and I applied for it, and was their number one candidate. I was offered, and accepted the City Manager job in their city, which was located only about a dozen miles away from New York City.

Several years later, I became dissatisfied with the job, my son was attending a college in New York City, so I drew a line around New York City, and applied for a City Manager job in Connecticut. When I was offered this job, I realized that I was relocating to a city in New England.

I like New England since it has a great sense of history, as being the first states in America. I still live here and enjoy it greatly!

When you live in New England for a while, you ultimately find out that there are two areas in New England – Northern New England (Maine, New Hampshire, and Vermont), and Southern New England (Connecticut, Massachusetts, and Rhode Island).

A public professional should relocate to a city/state wherever their family would like to go!

Political Party Affiliations

During my city management career, I changed my political party affiliations a few times for a number of reasons. Over the years, I registered as a Republican ®, a Democrat (D), and as an Unaffiliated Voter (UV). The reasons for these political party affiliations over the ears during my city management career were for the following reasons.

Early in my city management career, I was a registered Democrat (D) and, at one public meeting a city council member said to me that I heard that you were a Democrat, which makes me believe that you are a liberal, and now I know why you wish to help minority groups and senior citizens when we increase our program user fees for services. You always look for discounts for low-income citizens and senior citizens. This was his belief based on my personal political party affiliation.

Later in my city management career, I was a registered Republican (R) and at one public meeting a city council member said to me that I heard that you were a Republican, which makes me believe that you are a conservative, and now I know why you wish to keep our budget low, minimize our tax increases, and want all citizens to pay their respective share of our budget expenses. You always try to keep our budget low, and minimize our annual tax increases. This was his belief based on my personal political party affiliation.

I did not like these elected officials, my bosses as their City Manager, to think that I was making recommendations to them based on my political party affiliations. This was not how I liked the elected officials that appointed me to think about the recommendations that I made to them during my tenure as their City Manager.

So, later in my city management career, I changed my political party affiliation to that of an Unaffiliated Voter (UV), since this shows that I am an independent thinker, and that all of my recommendations to them were -professional in nature, and not political in nature.

From that point on, I reflected this philosophy about my political affiliation to all of the elected officials that I worked for. I even used these thoughts during future job interviews that I underwent for other City Management positions during my career.

The Cities elected officials were my boss, and I respected all of them, notwithstanding their respective personal political affiliations. If they are elected by majority vote, they represented the governing body that hired me and that I work for. I did what they wanted me to by their majority vote.

This political philosophy was held for the duration of my City Manager career, and I liked how everyone appreciated it. The bottom-line was that I have no political party affiliation, I am a working professional, and all of my recommendations to my elected officials are always only profession in nature.

All of the mayors and city council members that I worked for over the years have liked this professional perspective. After all, I respected all of them regardless of their own personal political party affiliation.

LESSON TWO

ELECTED OFFICIALS

How Mayors Are Elected

The process by which mayors are elected to office are contained in a City's Charter, which is usually voted upon by citizens when their city was formed. Such City Charters are revised now and then, when a city's elected officials vote to place a Charter Revision on their city's ballot for a special election.

Having been a City Manager in cities on both coasts of the United States, I can reflect upon how mayors receive their office in those cities that I served in as their City Manager.

These citizen mayoral selection processes are highlighted below:

— In one city that I was City Manager in, all political candidates ran for the city council, and the city council, by majority vote, appointed the mayor. The mayor's term of office, in the city that I worked in, was for one year. Since the term of office for city council members was four years, almost every city council member could be the mayor if they desired to serve in this capacity during their respective term of office.

— In another city that I worked in, no one ran for mayor, and the City Charter required that all candidates for public office could only run for a position on the city council, and that the candidate that ran for city council and received the most votes could be sworn-in as the city's mayor. If the number one vote-getter did not want to be the mayor, the next highest vote-getter could be the mayor if she or he wanted to.

— In another city that I worked in, a citizen would have to run for, and be elected to the position of mayor. A citizen had the option of running for either the elected position of mayor or as a member of the city council. The citizens voted to directly elect the mayor and city council members in this community.

These options reflect three different approaches for a citizen, if she or he wanted to become the mayor of their city, and they lived in one of these communities, to receive and hold this elected public office.

These laws vary from city to city in municipalities throughout our nation, based on the City Charter that was adopted by their respective citizens when their city was incorporated (initially formed).

Most citizens in America only know how "their" respective mayor is elected in the city that they live in, but there are other political processes that are available, depending upon a City's Charter, which was approved by the citizens when their city was legally formed.

All citizens should know that their City Charters must be consistent with their respective state's laws. If a City Charter is not, this portion of their voter-approved City Charter is invalid, since their state's laws must be followed by public officials cities at all times.

How Mayors Are Selected

The way a mayor is selected is highlighted in a City's Charter, which was approved by the citizens when the city was incorporated.

In the cities that I was a City Manager in, there were three processes by which a mayor was selected, and they are highlighted below.

- In one city that I worked in all city council candidates ran for the city council, and the person with the highest vote count was offered the opportunity to be the city's mayor for his/her term of office.
- In another city that I worked in, a candidate that wanted to be the city's mayor would run for this elected position. Whoever ran for this position, and got the most votes, became the city's mayor.
- In yet another city that I was a City Manager in, everyone seeking public office ran for the position of city council member. This city had five city council members, and they would vote for a new city mayor every year, since the term of office for the mayor's position was for one year.

In the city where everyone ran for the city council, the person with the highest number of votes, would hold this position for their term of office. If they wanted to hold this position again, they would have to run for the city council again and receive the highest number of votes.

In the city where candidates for the mayor position ran for this position, they would have a term of office, and could run for this position again in the future if they wished, but they would have to be the highest voter recipient again.

In the third city that I worked in, no one ran for the mayor position, but everyone ran for the city council, and the city council, by majority vote, would select one of their city council members to be the city mayor for one year. Since they each held four-year terms of office, this means that almost all of them could become the city's mayor during their term of office.

How a person is selected mayor varies greatly from city-to-city, and state-to-state. The examples that I presented above were based on City Manager experience in three states, a city in California, a city in New Jersey, and a city in Connecticut.

I would say that most citizens do not know how their mayor is selected, but they should. Two more major examples are, in the strong mayor form of government someone runs for the position of mayor, typically for a two-year term of office.

In the Mayor-Council form of government, it would be the same! In this form of municipal government, the mayor makes recommendations to his/her city council, and they must approve what the mayor wants to do by majority vote!

▌Maintaining A City's Public Infrastructure

It is important to properly maintain a city's public infrastructure. A city's elected officials, its mayor and city council, are responsible for doing this.

A newly paved street lasts about 25 years, and it is much cheaper to resurface them every eight to ten years, rather than have to fully replace them after a quarter of a century. A City Engineer once told me that repaving a street cost about one-third of the cost of having to reconstruct it.

May elected officials have different thoughts about saving funds to use to upgrade and replace their city's public infrastructure. I asked one mayor once if he would favor having a City Infrastructure Fund to save money annually to use on resurfacing our city's streets, so we did not have to reconstruct them when they wore out.

The mayor told me, I am only in my public office for about four years or so, and then I will no longer hold a public office in our city, so why should I care about having such a fund, since our public infrastructure won't wear out during my term-of-office.

This is how many elected officials think when it comes to increasing public taxes to create and finance a Public Instructure Fund of their city. Over the years, the maintenance and replacement of a city's public infrastructure is important, even thought it might not wear out until a few years down the road, so to speak.

I would normally get the mayor and city council to fund a Street Assessment Study, and hire a Traffic Engineer, to assess the state of City's streets, and categorize them by their respective age. Such a plan typically includes a city's major streets, and related public improvements, like street lights, traffic signals, sidewalks, and curbs.

While many mayors and city councils would approve funds for such a study, it was very difficult to get them to create a City Infrastructure Fund and finance it, to maintain their city's streets in future years.

In one city that I worked in, I got the mayor and city council to put funding for such a plan on the city's election ballot, and let their citizens vote on increasing their taxes to finance this service in future years. When the citizens voted on it, over ninety percent of them voted "no," since this was the general feeling of the public when it came to increase their taxes for this purpose.

As America's cities age, the next generation of a city's citizens will have to pay for this service. As our city streets wear out in future years, only time will tell if citizens change their mind about providing proper funding for the maintenance and upkeep of their city's public infrastructure!

▌ Job Interview Question — Annual Salary

I applied to be a City Manager in a specific city, and I was going through an interview process with their mayor and city council, and they asked me the following question.

The mayor asked me, if we offer you our City Manager position, what kind of an annual salary would you expect from us for serving in this position?

I responded that, I have no personal salary expectation, but that there is a national expectation, based upon various management studies, and how much money other City Manager's in our nation have been offered when they have accepted their respective City Manager positions.

I told them that the "rule of thumb" was that a management employee should receive, on the average, a salary of 10 percent more than the employees that they are managing.

I told them, that I personally did not care what my hiring salary was to be their new City Manager, but that I expected to make 10 percent more of a salary than their highest paid department manager.

I also told them that I did not care if this was $50,000, $75,000, or $100,000 and that I only wanted to make 10 percent more than their highest paid department manager.

The mayor immediately responded that, so you expect to make 10 percent more than their Chief of Police, that they should ask him to be their next City Manager.

The mayor responded, that he was not qualified to be our City Manager.

I, as an applicant for their City Manager position, said "Thank You!"

I don't recall hearing back from them, so I kept on applying for other City Manager positions throughout the nation.

Job Interview Question — Education

I was going through a job interview for a City Manager position with a city's mayor and city council. Each elected official reviewed every applicant's resume, and asked them questions about their respective work experience and educational background.

When it came to me for my interview, one of the questions asked to me by the city's mayor was, Roger, do we need a City Manager with a Doctoral Degree in Public Administration?

I promptly responded that my Ph.D. Degree in Public Administration was not related to my city management job. I said that I had some time left on the G.I. Bill a few years ago, and that I worked on and completed my doctoral degree since I like to teach graduate seminars in public administration at local universities in the evenings when I work full-time as a City Manager.

I explained that I have been a City Manager in a few cities, and that I have always taught in a graduate public administration program at a local university one night a week, and that my doctoral degree helped me be selected to serve as a faculty member for a university's adjunct faculty.

This degree has helped me teach graduate seminars at night, training young people to be future City Managers, and that it was an honor to teach such students based upon my work experience and educational background.

The mayor responded to my answer by saying "Thank you, Dr. Kemp."

The city council ultimately offered me the opportunity to be their future City Manager.

I subsequently became their City Manager, and also taught graduate seminars at a local public university in the evening during my tenure as their City Manager.

I felt that this combination of experience and education was good for the students.

It may also be good for the city and the citizens that I serve during my tenure as their City Manager.

Job Interview Question — Minorities

I was a finalist for a City Manager position in a very wealthy community, where rich people lived, and it was surrounded by other nice, but not so wealthy, communities.

When I went before the mayor and city council for my job interview for their City Manager position, I was asked the following city-related job interview question.

The mayor mentioned that their city has a few parks that are located on the boundary lines with some neighboring communities, and that they were having some problems, and wanted to know how I would resolve them.

The question was, some minorities come into their parks from neighboring communities, and some of them would go through the trashcans in their parks to take out plastic bottles and aluminum cans, since they would recycle them and get some money for doing so.

The mayor said, how would you correct this situation in our community's parks, so minorities would not want to come to them and go through the trashcans in these parks. Some of their citizens complained about this, and they wanted to know what I could do to correct this situation.

I responded to them that, you can't legally keep citizens out of your city parks, but that you could do the following, which other cities have done throughout our nation in similar circumstances.

— You could remove these trashcans from your city parks, and this would prevent people from coming to your parks and going through them to remove recyclable items.
— You could have two types of trashcans in your city parks, one for trash and another one for recyclable materials (e.g., like bottles and aluminum cans). The material placed in these recyclable cans could be removed by the city's staff during the day. This would preclude other folks from taking this material out of their respective containers, and recycling it for money.
— The third option would be to place a locked-lid on your recyclable cans, so that citizens could place glass and plastic bottles in them through a smaller hole in the top, but that the top of such refuse recycling containers would have a lock on it so that citizens could not open such containers and remove any of the recyclable material contained in them.

The mayor and city council liked my response, and I was happy about that, since my answer to this question would help my City Manager-interview process.

After the job interview, I returned tom my home, and later I thought that I might not want to live in a community that does not want minorities in their public parks, and wants their city staff to figure out ways to keep them out of their parks.

After some introspective reflection, I felt that I would not want to live in a city that had these values, since they were not consistent with my own personal values.

The Mayor's Letters

As a new City Manager, I thought that the mayor should sign all letters going out to Corporate Presidents of businesses in our community.

There were basically two types of these letters:

— *Welcome Letters* – When a new corporation moves to town, and we want to think them for moving to our community.
— *Code Violation Letters* – When a city employee sees a code violation, and we want to inform the President of the company about it so she/he could have it corrected.

The first couple of letters that went out to Corporate Presidents were *Welcome Letter,* which the mayor thanked me for preparing and immediately signed them, and they would be mailed out the same day.

The next few letters that went out to Corporate Presidents were *Code Violation Letters*, which the mayor reviewed, and called me to his office to say that he would sign all *Welcome Letters*, but he preferred that the City Manager should sign all *Code Violation Letters*.

The mayor's logic was that, as he explained it to me, since he is an elected official, he would like to sign all positive letters to Corporate Presidents (like *Welcome Letter*), but that he thinks that the City Manager should sign all negative letters to Corporate Presidents (like *Code Violation Letters*).

So, during my term of office, I prepared all *Welcome Letters* for the mayor to sign, and I prepared all *Code Violation Letters* for me to sign. This is how the political environment works, and reflects the difference between elected and appointed officials.

The Mayor's Question

I applied for the city Manager position in this community!

I was going through a City Manager job interview process a while back with the city's elected representatives – their mayor and city council.

I applied for this City Manager job because the city was located in a state that my family and I would not mind relocating to.

During my interview process with the mayor and city council, the mayor asked me the following unusual question.

The mayor said that I would be getting a city car, if I was appointed as their City Manager, and that this was usual, and I thought that it was great!

During my City Manager interview process, the mayor also said to me, and the city council was all around the interview table in their conference room, when their mayor posed the following question to me, which was a s follows.

Roger, since you are receiving a city car, I would suggest that if you ever pick-up a prostitute, that you never do this in a city car?

My response to the mayor was, since this was an unusual question, don't worry about me mayor, if I ever pick up a prostitute in our city, I promise that I will not use my city vehicle, but only my own personal car.

Then I asked the mayor and city council for their next question.

After this question, which I had never received during my entire city management career, I felt that the next topic should be – the next question from the mayor and city council please!

Then I asked for other City Manager job interview questions from their mayor and city council, and they were received during the remainder of my job interview process.

I was not a job finalist for this City Manager position in this city, and based on the mayor's question, I was very happy about this!

So, during the coming months, I applied for other City Manager positions in those cities that I thought that I would like to serve in during my City Management career.

Lunch with the Mayor

I was a City Manager, in a new city, and the mayor asked me to go out to lunch with him, which was a reasonable request, so I did.

We went to a nice local restaurant, we both had lunch, and talked, and had a great conversation about the city, our relationship, and how we were going to deal with the city council during the coming months.

It was a great lunch, a wonderful conversation that I had with the mayor, and then the mayor left our table for a few minutes, and when he did, I asked our waitress where the bill for our meal was?

She said that the "mayor never pays for his meals at our restaurant, and that when he brings his friends, that they never pay either – so there will be no bill coming, since all of you get to eat for free."

The owner of the restaurant said they liked the mayor coming to his restaurant, and that the more and more people that see the mayor in his restaurant, that they tell their friends about this, and that more and more citizens come to this restaurant to eat meals because of this all of the time.

So, when the mayor returned, I did not mention anything about the bill for our meal, but I just thanked the mayor for taking me out to lunch, and I told him that I wanted to leave the tip for our waitress for her great service, which I did. I left her a tip that was equal to the price of the meal that I had for lunch.

I thanked the mayor for the great lunch, and the mayor thanked me for leaving the tip, and we both went back to work. I went back to city hall, and he went back to the company that he worked at.

I felt that the mayor was honored for getting a free meal at this restaurant, since the more citizens that saw him there brought in more and more citizens who wished to have a meal at this restaurant.

So, I felt that I did the right thing in leaving the tip for our waitress, since I paid for my lunch and she got a great tip!

The Grant Application

When I was a relatively new City Manager, the mayor called me into his office and gave me a Grant Application. He said that in the past, the City Manager had given this Grant Application to another city employee to complete, and the City Manager would return it to the mayor for his signature to make the official application for this grant.

I told the mayor I would take it home and read the Grant Application and that I would get back to him the next day if I had any comments. Otherwise, I would give it to another employee to complete, then return it to the mayor for his signature so that our city could submit the official Grant Application.

When I reviewed the Grant Application that evening, I noticed that the Grant, an Economic

Development Grant, was for cities with a population of 60,000 or more. Smaller cities would not qualify for this Grant.

The next day I met with the mayor about this Economic Development Grant, and I told him that it was only for cities that had a population of 60,000 or more, and that we would not qualify since our city's population was only one-half of this amount, about 30,000 citizens.

The mayor told me that he knew that we did not qualify for this Grant, but that he liked to apply for it anyway. The reason why, he said, was that when he signed the Grant Application and officially applied for it, that he would give a copy of the Grant Application to the local newspaper.

The local newspaper, he said, would then put a story of the city applying for this Economic Development Grant on their newspaper's front page, and that they would always include a picture of the mayor on the front page too. He said that he liked this, since it helped increase his popularity, and that it would help him get re-elected to his office during the coming election.

Since I could understand the mayor's thinking, I personally completed the Grant Application, since it would not be fair to our taxpayers if they paid to have one of our employees do this work. Also, I completed this Grant Application at home, so it was done on my time, and the taxpayers did not have to pay any one for doing this work.

When I returned the Grant Application to the mayor for his signature, he thanked me! I told him that it was my pleasure to fill out this Economic Development Grant Application for him. The mayor told me that he would sign it, apply for this Grant, and deliver a copy to our local newspaper for their front-page story.

About a week later, on the front page of our local newspaper, there was a large article about the city applying for this Economic Development Grant, and next to the story was a nice picture of the mayor.

It was not wrong for the mayor to want to apply for this Grant, but I was glad that I did this work at home on my own time, since he got the results that he expected for his application for this Economic Development Grant, but it did not cost our taxpayers anything!

Professional administrators think differently then elected officials, but they are appointed by them. I think that I did the right thing!

The Mayor's Parking Tickets

I worked in one city where the mayor who, like most mayors, was frequently asked to give a speech before a local social or civic organization. Most cities have many of these organizations, and mayors like to speak to them, since it increases their 'local' popularity.

This one day, the mayor came to see me and told me that he was going to give a speech, and was running late, so he illegally parked and then went into the building where the group that invited him was having their meeting. H said that he made it on time, and was glad since many citizens were in this room waiting to hear him give his speech.

When he left, and returned to his car to come back to city hall, he noticed that he had a parking ticket. Upon returning to city hall, he gave me the parking ticket and asked me to "fix-it" since he was the mayor, was running late to give a speech, and it was not his fault. He instructed me to ask our chief of police to handle this.

I thought about the mayor's parking ticket, and realized that if the chief of police "fixed-it," and if anyone told the local newspaper, that it could wind-up on the front page! For this reason, and since I had never "fixed" a parking ticket before, I decided that night, when I was at home, that I would pay this ticket myself. So, I made out a check, and placed it in the envelope that the mayor received with the parking ticket, stamped the envelope, and mailed it in on behalf of the mayor.

I was glad that such parking tickets only required a $10. Payment, since the mayor received about one parking ticket a month, and gave each one to me to have it "fixed." I would always take the mayor's parking ticket home, write a $10. Check to pay it, and mail in this payment for the mayor.

I was happy that this mayor was not re-elected; and I never had to pay any parking tickets for any other mayor in my life that I worked for as a City Manager.

I feel that I did the right thing, no one knew the disposition of the mayor's parking tickets, except me, and the mayor was happy that he only had to give his parking tickets to me, and I would take care of them!

Also, the mayor was always my friend during his term of office!

Mayor Wanted to See Me

In one of my City Manager positions, after a couple of years, the mayor asked to see me, so I went to his office, and he related the following information.

He said that some of the members of the city council don't like you, and that they wanted me to look for another job, so that they would not have to terminate me.

I asked the mayor if this viewpoint was held by a majority of our city council members, or just a few of them. He said that some of them don't like you, but after the next election this could change.

I told the mayor that my employment contract with the city notes that they could terminate me at any time, but that they would have to give me a year's salary under my employment contract with the city that they approved when I was hired.

He said that the ones that don't like you, do not want to pay you a year's salary if they terminate you, because of the level of city money that would be involved in this termination process.

I thanked the mayor for his comments, and said that I will wait for the next election to see if a majority of the city council members don't like me, and if they would like to terminate my employment with the city.

In the meantime, I started looking for another job, and within six months, I was offered another City Manager position in a city that was twice the size of the city that I was managing, and the salary that they offered me was twice as much as the salary that I was receiving in my present City Manager position.

I'm learning about politics, and am glad that I was so qualified that I could apply for another job, go through the city's City Manager interview process, and be selected for another City Manager position. The city I was asked to serve in was twice as large and the salary that was offered was double of the one that I was currently receiving.

I wrote a letter of resignation to the mayor and city council, and I was happy to leave my position for a salary that was twice the salary that I was making with them. I was moving on to a new City manager position and that would help my city management career.

After I left this city, a few weeks later, I read the local regional newspaper that the mayor was quoted as saying that I was the best City Manager that their city ever had, and that he hated to see me go!

I felt that I've been learning a lot about local politics, and that I was learning more about this process based on the mayor's recent comments. My application and selection into the new City Manager position in a city that was twice as large, and paid twice as much money as they did was the right move.

I felt that, while I am not a politician, that I am highly qualified City Manager, I did the right thing – since some of these city council members did not like me, and they were glad to see me go.

And, more importantly, that I was glad to go to a city twice as large, and make twice as much money – which would greatly help my City Manager career for years to come!

LESSON THREE

APPOINTED OFFICIALS

Preparation for City Manager Job Interview

During my public service career, when I applied for a City Manager job, I would always arrive in the city that I was being interviewed in for this position, at least a day early, so I could properly prepare myself for my upcoming interview with the city's mayor and city council.

During this pre-interview time, I would always do two things that were relatively simple to do, yet they would make me highly informative about certain important municipal topics.

The two things that I would always do are as follows:

— I would go downtown to a local eatery (for breakfast, lunch, or dinner), and would try to sit at a counter at a local café or restaurant. I wanted to be close to people, so I could informally ask them some questions.

The questions I would ask them would be, re you pleased with your police department's services in your downtown area, and are citizens generally pleased with the local property taxes that they must pay?

— I would also go to the city's public library, sometimes for several hours, to become educated on the following topics.

The first thing I would do is ask the librarian where I could see the city's annual budget, since a city's local public library always had a hard-copy of their annual budget for citizens to review. I would see how their revenues and expenses were aligned, and how much their budget was increasing from year to year.

Also, I would ask the librarian if I could see the city's annual audit, so I could see all of their funds, their balances, and see if the city's audit had any "findings" or made any "recommendations."

The last thing I would do would be to ask the librarian where I could see copies of the city's local newspaper. I would go back a few months, review any city stories on their front page, and look to see if there were any newspaper articles about problems that the city was having.

This helped me become educated about the city, its annual budget process, the status of its funding levels and reserve accounts, and about any local issues that were facing the city. This was time well spent for a job application for their city's City Manager position.

Usually, after a City Manager job interview process was over, I would always be one of the top-three finalists for their City Manager position. This led me to believe that I was doing the right thing in my City Manager job interview preparation process.

Nowadays, much of this information is on a city's website. Frequently, highlights of their budget are on their website, and sometimes even their entire annual budget. Also, some cities even post their annual audit on their website. This would help city manager job applicants before they even arrive in the city for their job interview.

My First City Manager Job

When I worked in my first city, I attended a local university in the evening while working full-time, using the remainder of the G.I. Bill that I was entitled to after my military service in the U.S. Coast Guard.

I was an Assistant to the City Manager and I was applying for Assistant City Manager position, primarily throughout the state that I lived in. When I talked to a local city manager, he told me not to do this for the following reason.

He said that a City Manager would not like to hire you as an Assistant City Manager, since you now have a Ph.D. degree in Public Administration, and that he/she would think that you would want, or could get, their job since they probably would not have an advanced graduate degree like you do.

I agreed with this seasoned city manager, and I stared applying for city manager positions.

I kept on getting more-and-more city manager job interviews during the coming months.

Within several months, I was selected to go through a city manager job interview with a mayor or city council, along with several other city manager job applicants.

I went through this job interview process, became a city manager job finalist, and completed some final interviews with other city manager job finalist for this position.

After this process, I was unanimously selected by this city's mayor and city council to be their new city manager.

This meant that, while I worked in my previous city for about five years, that the same month that I received my Ph.D. degree in Public Administration that I was selected to be a city manager!

I was proud, and this new position was my first city manager position during my quarter-of-a-century plus management career. A career that encompassed both the east and west coasts of the United States.

It was a great career, and I was glad that I attended night school for five years in my first position as a city manager. The doctoral degree in public administration that I received during that time facilitated my public service career for many years to come!

Applying for a Job in a Wealthy Community

A national-recruiter called me up, and asked me to apply for the city manager job of one of the wealthiest, high-income communities, in America.

Since I could double my salary, I applied for the job, and was selected to go through the employment interview process with this city's mayor and city council.

I looked around the community for a few days before my job interview. Since the city manager had to live in the city, I looked at houses, and the cheapest one I could find was a World War II Cape Cod home. It had a for sale sign on it, and I called the realtor with this listing, and she said that this home was for sale for $1.3 million.

I then went through the job interview, and the city council informed me that none of their city government's employees had to live in their city, but that the city manager had to, since this was an employment requirement that was in their city charter.

I told them that I looked around at "cheap houses" and the cheapest one I could find on the market was for sale for $1.3 million. I told them that I could not afford to purchase this home.

The mayor and city council told me not to worry about it, since they would buy the hone for their new city manager, deed it to him/her, and they would own it This would satisfy the city's requirement that their city manager must live in their city.

They said that when the city manager leaves their city, that he/she would sell the house and have to pay them back the amount that the city paid to purchase the house for them when they started their job. They also said that the city manager had to stay there a minimum of three years.

I thought that this was an unusual city charter requirement, so I backed-out of the job interview process to become the next city manager of this very wealthy city.

City Manager Job Requirements

When the previous city manager left his/her position for another job in a neighboring city, I was asked by the city's mayor if I would like to be their Acting City Manager. I was a career city manager, but I had left my previous position to be a Practitioner in Residence at a local university.

I accepted, since I was a Practitioner in Residence teaching graduate seminars in the evenings at a local university, and that my daytimes were free. I also explained to the mayor that I would continue to teach in the evenings if there were no meetings or other work requirements.

So, I started in this new city manager position, and after several months, the mayor and the city council liked me, and the mayor asked me if I would like to accept this job permanently, but that the city charter required that I live in their city. It was a legal requirement!

I thought about it, and thought that this was a strange, old-fashioned, legal requirement for the following reasons:

- I lived in a neighboring community, that was about a mile from their city line,
- I could drive-to-work in less than ten minutes,
- I lived closer to their city hall than citizens that lived in their city,
- I lived in a house with a mortgage that was almost paid off,
- I thought about buying a condominium in their city but this did not make any sense,
- Since it would cost a lot of money that there was no need to spend such money.

So, I explained these things to their mayor, and he said that the law was (i.e., their city charter) that I legally had to live in their city once I was appointed as their city manager.

After all these laws vary from state-to-state. In some states if you can drive to work within one-half hour, you can legally live in any neighboring community – so long as you can make it to work within this timeframe.

Many city charters are old, and it would take an election, and vote of their citizens, to change such a city charter legal requirement – so such changes are seldom made for this reason.

I told the mayor that I would continue to serve as their Acting City Manager until they did a formal recruitment, and found someone to take my place, and then voted to fill this position.

So, this is what I did do, and they filled the position, then I went back to teaching more graduate seminars as a Practitioner in Residence at a local university.

City charters are old, some are strange, and they can be changed by a majority vote of a city's citizens – so everyone usually follows their respective city charters since it is a time-consuming and expensive process to undertake to legally change them.

City Managers and Economic Development

When I was invited to an interview to be the city's new city manager, I would also look at possible economic development opportunities in their city before my interview with their mayor and city council.

I would arrive a day or so early, and would drive around their downtown area, and surrounding neighborhoods, and look for various available economic development opportunities.

Such economic development opportunities would typically include;

- Likely vacant sites that could be developed,
- Other sites with old vacant buildings on them,
- Contaminated sites that could be redeveloped,
- Site that could be combined to be developed, and
- Other economic development opportunities.

I would also check to see what Economic Development Grants were provided by their State to stimulate economic development within the cities in their state.

When economic development takes place, the city gets the property taxes from the sites that are developed, and this is a wonderful revenue source!

Also, the state gets the income taxes from the salaries that are paid to the new company's employees!

Both of these revenue sources – the property tax and the income tax, go on forever for both these levels of government and promote economic development –the city and their state.

If a site was previously developed, and a developer wishes to develop a site for business, they would want a clean site that is ready to develop. They do not want to have to pay to clean it up to do this, since they would rather purchase a clean site.

So, if their state has a grant available to clean-up contaminated sites, and make them clean for redevelopment, then both levels of government –city and state, stand to benefit from such redevelopment projects for years to come.

Knowing what vacant sites might be available for this purpose, would help me greatly during mt city manager job interview with a city's mayor and city council.

Also, since other city manager applicants finalists usually did not do this, it would give me a distinct advantage to talk about this important topic with a city's mayor and city council.

My answers to these questions would sometimes help me be a city's number-one city manager applicant for their city manager position.

This was a great subject to use to prepare for a job interview for a city manager position!

Contract Labor Attorney Services

In most cities that I have worked in as a city manager, the city would contract out legal services to get a Labor Attorney to negotiate on their behalf.

This would be expensive, but well worth the price, since each major city employee union would usually have their own contract Labor Attorney. They would be a well experienced attorney in the field of city-union labor negotiate.

One time between labor negotiation sessions, the City's Contract Labor Attorney went to Florida on vacation. When he returned, I got a legal services bill from the attorney's office that he worked for. The bill was for his services to my city for the past month.

I noticed on this bill that there were a few charges billed to the city for some of the time that he had spent in Florida. So, I called up this attorney, and asked him how his firm could bill my city for some of the time that he was on vacation in Florida, and that this bill needs to be corrected.

He responded, when I go on vacation, I always bring some of my labor negotiation work with me, and in this case, it was several documents and union contracts from your city. He said that, I just don't lay on the beach when I am on vacation, I do work and, when I do, I keep track of it and my legal company bills our clients for it!

He made a good point, since he charged my city by the for the labor negotiations work that he does for us, regardless of where he is when he does this work for us. In this case he was on vacation in Florida.

While city manager's don't get paid by the hour when they are on vacation, Contract Labor Attorney's do!

The Best Way to Hire Department Managers

When a city department manager retires, or leaves the city for another position, I would always use the following department manager selection process, which worked very well over the years, in every city that I served as its City Manager.

I would typically appoint the employee closest to the Department Manager, as the Acting Department Manager. When the department manager retired, or left her/his position for another one, then I would undertake a recruitment process to find a new Department Manager.

The advertisement for a new Department Manager position would be placed in both state and national publications, including the appropriate professional association publications, since each of them typically ran recruitment advertisements.

Applicants would apply for this job, and the qualifications for this position would be placed in the advertisement for it. The human Resources Department staff would save these applications for the next step in the Department Manager recruitment process.

For each selection process, I would check with similar Department Manager in other communities in our region. They would have to have an excellent reputation, be respected professionally within our state, and be from a city that was about the same size as ours, since these department managers would be performing services in a community that was about the same size as the one that I worked in.

1. They would review all of the applications for this position, and pick the best applicants based on the applicant's respective qualifications.
2. I would ask them to select the top five best candidates for this Department Manager position.
3. When they all agreed on the top five Department Manager candidates, the City's Human Resources Management staff would set-up interview for the top-five applicants.
4. I would ask the Department Manager selected to serve on this Department Manager Selection Committee to interview the top five applicants for this position, then to give me the names of the "top three" candidates, and I would interview each of them personally, and select the best one to be our city's next Department Manager.

I would explain this process to the mayor and city council, and they would always agree that I was doing the right thing.

In this Department Manager Selection Process, I would get the, top -three names of the finalists for this position, and personally interview them, and hire one of them to be our next Department Manager.

This was not a political process, but merely a professional selection process where other respected Department Managers would pick the finalists that I would interview for our city's position!

The Library Director

In almost every city that I worked in, the City Manager was responsible for appointing all department managers, including the Library Director.

In a couple of cities that I worked in, the Library Department had its own appointed or elected Board of Trustees or Board of Directors. These respective boards had the responsibility for hiring the Library Director, and terminating the Library Director, if they thought it was appropriate.

In on city on the West Coast, the City's Charter noted that the Library Department was an Independent Special District, directed by a Board of Trustees, and that they were elected by the citizens of the community. They were responsible for appointing the Library Director.

In the other city on the East Coast, the City's Charter noted that the Library Department was a department of the city, but was directed by a Board of Directors, that were appointed by the City Council. So, these Library Board members were appointed by the City Council, and not elected by the citizens. They were also responsible for appointing the Library Director.

These elected and appointed members of their respective Library Board, held monthly meetings, that the Library Director attended, not the City Manager.

I got along well with these Board-appointed Library Directors, since they were professional in nature, and most of them had an MLS (Master of Library Science) degrees, and were respected professionals in their field.

In this type of arrangement, the respective Board of Trustees and Board of Directors for each library were politically neutral, and just wanted to make sure that their city had a good Library Department that provided quality services to their citizens.

Library Directors, as well as citizens, frequently told me that their city did this with the goal of keeping city politics out of the library's management and operations. They all wanted their respective public libraries to be professional in nature, and provide quality services to the citizens of their respective communities.

Professional Department Managers

In one of the city's that I was a City Manager in, a Department Manager retired and, when he did so, he proved that the Council-Manager form of Government is much better than other forms of municipal government.

The reasons for this are as follows:

- If a mayor, in a strong mayor form of government, appoints a department manager, she/he usually lasts as long as the mayor does in his/her term of office.
- After all, a newly elected mayor would not want the old mayor's department manager to service under him/her, the newly elected mayor.
- Also, in a Mayor-Council form of Municipal Government a mayor can appoint any department manager that she/he would like to, but it must be approved by the City Council.

In a City Council-Manager for of Government, the city manager appoints all department managers, and they serve in their respective positions for a much longer time then they do in other forms of local government.

In a previous City Manager position that I held, the Planning Director retired, and the city was holding a retirement party/dinner for him, since he had served in the city for more than 35 years.

During this departments manager's tenure, for nearly a third of a century, he served under several mayors, and few city managers.

He was a professional, did a good job, and held his position under this form of government for many years, and the citizens welcomed him to do so, since he was a true professional.

This would not happen in different forms of government. In a strong—mayor form of government, a newly elected mayor would want to appoint a new Planning Director.

In a Mayor-Council form of government, a mayor needs the approval of the City Council to appoint a new department manager, like a Planning Director.

In a Council-Manager form of government, the City Manager appoints all department managers, and they serve in their respective positions so long as they are competent, and they only leave when they wish to retire, or move on to another job.

So professional department managers can serve a much longer time under the Council-Manager for of government, then if they were appointed by the mayor under a different form of local government.

This fact always helped me enjoy the form of local government that I worked in, the Council-Manager form, since professionals were present – and they could serve in their respective jobs as long as they wanted to.

Doing the Right Thing

I had applied for a City Manager job in another city, and was interviewed, along with other applicants, for this position.

A few weeks later the mayor called me up and told me that I was a finalist and that the city council would like me to come again to their city for a follow-up interview.

I went through the second interview with the may and city council, and then flew back home after this job interview.

A week later the mayor called me up and said that I was the person that their city council wanted to hire, and we discussed my salary requirement and starting date. Sounds like we had a deal, and that I would be their next City Manager.

Then the mayor said, at the end of this telephone conversation, don't forget that during your first six months of employment with us that the City Council and I would like you to fire our Finance Direct and Chief of Police.

I asked the mayor, why? He said that the City's elected officials, their mayor and city council, were my boss, and I served them, and that most of them wanted me to do this. It was a part of my employment agreement with the mayor that I would do this.

I thanked the mayor for the telephone call, and told him that I would think about this initial job requirement, and get back to him in the next few days.

In a typical city the city manager determines who to hire and fire, not the mayor and city council. Because of this, I felt that a true professional would not take a job like this, since the mayor's request was political in nature, and I know nothing about the details of why they wanted these major department heads fired during my first six months of office.

I then called the mayor back, and told him that I had another job offer, and that I no longer had an interest in being their next City Manager.

I think that I am a professional City Manager, and that I did the right thing.

I followed-up and six months later and their new city manager had fired their Chief of Police and Finance Director. It was on the front page of their local newspaper, that the first thing the mayor and city council did was to fire their new city manager for doing this.

I did the right thing and was proud of it!

LESSON FOUR

POLITICS OF CITY GOVERNMENTS

The Location of Polling Places

When I was appointed as a new City Manager, I would always check with the appropriate members of the city staff to find out where the city polling places were located.

In some cities that I worked in over the years the location of polling places evolved over time to be located in various churches, and in the offices/buildings of various non-profit organizations, that were located in residential neighborhoods throughout the city.

I always felt that as a professional City Manager that polling places should be located in politically neutral locations, and I would always have them relocated, with city council approval, to city facilities, such as:

- Neighborhood Schools,
- Public Libraries,
- Park and Recreation offices, and
- City Hall.

Citizens always knew where the polling places in their neighborhoods were located, since they would all be located at local city public facilities, as described above.

Most cities also have a law that requires that no politicians, or their supporters, could hold a political sign within 75 or 100 feet from a polling place location. I would also have the Chief of Police have a police officer stand-by these polling locations on election days to make sure that this law was followed.

Cities also have laws that politicians can't place their political signs on city property, like on the side of roadways, in neighborhood parks, or on any other city facilities. I would also have the Chief of Police have a police officer look for these political sign violations prior to election day, and he could let me know their locations.

I would contact and tell the politicians running for office to remove their signs from public property immediately, or that I will send out the city staff to do this, and that they will receive a bill from us for providing this service.

I felt that this was the professional, politically neutral, practice to follow prior to and on election day at the city's polling places, and removing illegal signs from public property.

City with Large Minority Population

In my first City Manager job I was appointed by the mayor and city council of. City with a relatively large minority population. Overall, the city had a population that was about 60 percent non-minority, and about 40 percent minority.

I wanted to get along well with everyone, regardless of their gender, age, political affiliation, or whether or not they were anon-minority or minority. This was the employment goal in my first City Manager position.

This city also had a local chapter of the National Association for the Advancement of Colored

People (NAACP), which I respected, and I wanted to introduce myself to their President, and get to know him.

After checking out who their President was, I found out that he was a local dentist, so I called up his office and made an appointment with him. I was new to this city and I picked him as my personal dentist.

When I went to his office, I introduced myself as the city's newly appointed City Manager, and said that I looked forward to meeting him, since he was a respected dentist and the President of our city's NAACP Chapter.

When he was done with my dental appointment, I mentioned that if he agreed that good and bad people came in all colors. He said that he agreed with this philosophy, and that he was glad that I did too.

He became my dentist during my tenure in this city as their City Manager. If I ever had minority problems that was related to the NAACP Chapter, or I felt could be resolved by it, I would contact him.

He was always easy to work with, and I enjoyed having him as a friend during my first job as a City Manager.

I knew that I did the right thing, and was proud of it, and he was happy to meet me and to be my friend. He said that no other city manager had ever done this before, and he respected my efforts to reach out to him!

We worked well together during my tenure as their City Manager!

Citizen Complaints About Employees

Sometimes citizens would call me up, as their City Manager, and complain about some city employees. Some of these citizen complaints, which I always responded to, are highlighted below.

—   One citizen called me to let me know that one of our employees was a homosexual, and he did not want to pay this person's salary, since he was one of our taxpayers. He went on to state that this employee is single, and no women ever went to his house, only others males do, and this is why he knows that he is a homosexual.

—   Another citizen called me to let me know that one of our employees was an alcoholic, since he was always drunk when he was at home, and he saw all of the liquor bottles each week in the trash cans at his home.

—   A few years later, another citizen called me to let me know that he saw one of our city employees smoking a marijuana cigarette and, as a taxpayer, he did not like paying his salary and wanted me to have him arrested, and then fired.

In the first complaint, I checked out this employee, and his department manager said that he was one of his best departmental employees. He always reported to work on time, did a great job, and never left early, and frequently stayed late before he went home.

In the second complaint, I checked out this employee, and his department manager said that he was one of his best departmental employee. He always reported to work on time, did a great job, and never left early, and frequently stayed late before he went home.

In the third complaint, I checked out this employee, and his department manager said that he was one of his best departmental employees, and that he never smoked marijuana at work and, if he did, that he would be fired, since this is against the law.

I called back these three citizens and told them that what an employee does at home, is his/her personal business, and I am only concerned about their performance during their working hours with the city.

I called back the third citizen that complained about one of our employees smoking marijuana at home and, after checking with the City Attorney, I called back this citizen and said that if you ever see this employee doing this again just call our Police Department, and they will respond, and if he is caught smoking marijuana, that he would be arrested.

Citizens call now and then to complain about City employees, but a City Manager must respond to such enquiries properly, and should check with the City Attorney, before responding to some citizen complaints.

Over the years, I always did the right thing, but always checked with our City Attorney before responding to some of our citizens!

▎Altering an Employee Union Agreement

I was a newly appointed City Manager, and the Mayor and City Council had just changed, in the last election, from somewhat liberal to more conservative. The mayor told me that the new City Council wanted me to change some City requirements in one of the Employee Union Agreements.

I checked with the City Attorney, who said that the Employee Union Agreement approved by the previous City Council is a legal document, and that it was signed by the Mayor and the Employee Union President, after the City Council and the members of the Union had voted to approve it.

The City Attorney told me that I could ask the President of the Employee Union to reopen negotiations to renegotiate some of the items in their employment agreement with the City, and if he agreed to do this, then we could legally renegotiate changes to the previously approved City Council Employee Labor Union Agreement.

I went to the President of the Employee Union, and he told me that the Union did not want to do this, since the City Council had changed, and that their Union's employees were happy with this agreement, and did not want to change it in any way.

So, this was a three-year City-Employee Union Agreement and, because the Employee Union did not want to reopen City-Employee Union labor negotiations, I would have to wait for an additional two-plus years to do this. This was the law, and I had no choice!

I went back to the mayor and told him this, and he did not like this response, and he said that the City Council wanted me to change portions of the city-Employee Union Agreement. I told him again, that the Employee Union did not want to reopen labor negotiations, and that the City legally had no choice but to follow the law, the existing labor agreement, in this regard.

The mayor went on to blame me for not doing what the City Council wanted me to do. I told him that this was a legal matter, and that the City Attorney advised me that I could not do this.

The mayor did not like me after this exchange, yet I am a professional City Manager and I had no choice but to follow the law, which was to implement the previous City-Employee Labor Agreement approved by the former City Council.

I had no choice, and I did the right thing, but the Mayor and City Council did not like my course of action on their request, even thought it was the only legal option that I could follow.

Problems like this arise in city governments all the time, and a professional City Manager, like myself, has no options but to do what is the legally correct thing to do. I am a professional City Manager, and I knew that I did the right thing!

Police Access to a Military Base

The Chief of Police came to see me one day, and told me that on occasion one of his Police Officers would be pursuing someone that committed a crime, and this person would drive on to the Military Base, but that the Police Officers were stopped at the Military Base entrance gate, and told that they could not come on to the Federal property.

So, the Chief of Police was mad because his Police Officers could not pursue a military person that committed a violation of the law on to the Military Base. His Police Officers were always stopped by Military Guards at the entranceways to the base.

I agreed with the Chief of Police that this was not right, and that I would look into how to correct this situation. I then called up the Military Base Commander, who was a General, and made an appointment to meet him to discuss this issue.

This was a large Military Base adjacent to the city that I was City Manager of. It was not right that a military person could commit a crime in my city, and our Police Officers could not pursue them on to the military base, either to write them a ticket or arrest them, as appropriate.

I went to meet the General, and I introduced myself as the City Manager of the adjacent community. He introduced himself as the Commanding Officer of the Military Base. It was a large military base, legally on Federal property, with a couple thousand soldiers assigned to it.

I explained the problem to the Commanding Officer, and he told me that if this situation ever happened again to call him and let him know, and that he would contact his Gate Guards so that they would allow our Police Officers to immediately pursue the military person in the car that just drove into the Military Base.

When this happened again, I just called the General, and he made arrangements for quick access to the Military Base by our Police Officers. The Chief was happy, our Police Officers were pleased, and this case was closed1

Police Officer Salary Increases

I worked as the City Manager in one City where the Mayor and City Council gave the members of the City's Police Union, our Police Officers, a very small salary increase for two years in a row, with an adjustment of about two-to-three percent a year.

At this time, the annual inflation rate was between five and seven percent a year, so our Police Officers received an annual salary adjustment that was about on-half of what the inflation rate was.

The City's Police Union, consisting of all of our Police Officers, did not like this, and started taking actions to remove some of our City Council members, with the goal of getting some new City Council members that would give them a larger salary adjustment in the future.

It was election time, so this was a good time for our Police Officers to change the nature of our City's City Council. One thing that was difficult to deal with was that this was a very nice, and expensive, community to live in, and many of our Police Officers lived in our city.

Even though most of these Police Officers did not live in the city, they did the following things to try   to educate the public about their problem, with the goal of removing the current City Council members and getting new City Council members that would give them a larger salary adjustment in the future.

The political actions that they did include the following:

– Placing advertisements in local newspapers to promote their City Council candidates,
– Placing messages to citizens on a few large billboards in our city, and
– Knocking on doors, on their own off-duty time, to try to influence our citizens voting preferences.

These political efforts continued for a couple of months before the City's election. When the election was held, most of the City Council members that voted to give our Police Officer a low salary adjustment were removed from office.

The new City Council members were sworn-in, and took office with a positive attitude toward our City's Police Officers. During the following year's labor negotiations with the Police Union, the new City Council gave our Police Officers a ten-to-twelve present salary adjustment for two years.

This action made-up for their previous low salary adjustments, and proved that you do not have to live in a town to have an influence on its political process. While few Police Officers lived in town, they managed to change the outcome of our city's election, since their City Council candidates got elected.

I thought that this was good for our Police Officers, and I appreciated the fact that the City Council gave me the same salary increase that they provided to our Police Officers!

The City's Police Officers created this new political environment, which changed the nature of our City Council for years to come!

Police Officers and Computers

When I was in one City as a City Manager, every Police Officer had a laptop computer, and they all used them daily – when responding to crimes, doing research on criminals, and when they prepared their police reports. This was a great state-of-the-art Police Department practice from a computer standpoint.

Roger L. Kemp

In the next City where I was a City Manager no Police Officers had a laptop computer, and none of them ever used them because they never had them and they were never trained to use them. This was not good, and I needed to work with the Chief of Police so our Police Officers could learn how to use state-of-the-art technology on their job, like laptop computers.

Since I was a new City Manager, I went to meet with the Chief of Police about this situation, which I thought was a problem. I asked what was going on, and why weren't our Police Officers trained to use computers, and why weren't they using laptop computers like other Police Officers in cities throughout our nation are doing?

He responded to me that he personally did not like some new technologies, that he did not like computers, and that he did not want his (our City's) Police Officers to be using them. I thought about this, and then asked the Chief of Police, since he had been with the city for many years, how many more years he planned to be with the city until he retired?

He responded that he planned to retire in three years, and I told him that if he retired in one year, then I would not have to fire him – since I, as the City's new City Manager, wanted our Police Officers to be trained to use computers when they did their daily police jobs. After a brief time, the Chief of Police said that he would retire in one year, and then I could hire a new Chief of Police.

I thanked the Chief very much, he retired a year later, I hired a new Police Chief, and within six months our Police Officers were all using laptop computers on a daily basis to do their respective police duties.

The Chief of Police had a great career, retired with honor, and I hired a new Chief of Police to take his place, and the city became state-of-the-art from a computer standpoint. I feel that as the City's new City Manager, I did the right thing.

The Chief of Police had. Retirement party with our city, and I personally congratulated him for being our City's Chief of Police for so many years!

Police Discounts at a Local Restaurant

Some merchants gave some City employees a discount if they ate at their respective restaurants. I only saw this once, but I thought I would check it out as the City's New City Manager, since I had never seen this before in any other cities.

The owner of a local restaurant, as a Police Officer left his restaurant, said to the Police Officer that I give all Police Officers a ten percent discount, since I like them coming to my restaurant to eat. This Police Officer, like all others do, paid his bill and left to go back to work.

Since I was the next in line, I asked the owner of this restaurant why he gave our Police Officers a discount, and he responded. "My restaurant is not located in the best part of town, and if citizens driving by my restaurant sees Police cars in our parking lot, then more and more of these citizens top to eat here since they feel that our restaurant is a safe place."

He went on to state that he liked this, since nothing else, like citizens seeing Police cars in his parking lot, would bring in additional citizens who, once they see these Police cars, felt safer coming into his restaurant for. Meal.

I mentioned this to our Chief of Police, and I asked him if he cared that merchants such as this were giving discounts to our City's Police Officers. The Chief said that his Police Officers did not ask for this discount, it was merely the owner of the restaurant, who wanted citizens to see more Police cars in this restaurant's parking lot.

The primary beneficiary of this discount offer was the owner of this restaurant, and that Police Officers just parked their Police cars in his parking lot, and went there to eat because they liked the food at this restaurant.

I agreed with the Chief, that this was not a wrong thing for our Police Officers to be receiving a ten percent discount for eating at this restaurant, since they did not solicit it, and that they were just receiving it from the owner of this restaurant, since he wanted their Police cars in his restaurant's parking lot.

The more Police cars in his restaurant's parking lot, the more citizens dropped by his restaurant, and the more money he made. I did not feel that this was a bad thing, even though I always like to eat at this restaurant too, but that I never received such a discount!

There was no one to blame here except the owner of the restaurant, and he felt that he was doing the right thing, since he was making more money when Police Officers ate at his restaurant.

Things like this, offered by the restaurant's owner, probably take place in cities throughout America!

Invited to Speak to Church Leaders

The City's church leaders, which included preachers and pastors, and other church administrators, meet at City Hall periodically.

They were meeting this time at City Hall since they asked the mayor a question about City services and wanted an answer at their next monthly meeting.

The question was, all of their church parking lots are paved, but were many years old, and they all needed to be resurfaced, to make it easier for members of their respective congregations to park their cars when they attend their church services.

The mayor explained this question to me prior to this meeting, and wanted me to attend their next meeting at City Hall to answer this question for them. The mayor said that he would be there to accompany me.

I went to their next meeting at City Hall, which was being held in a conference room right down the hall from my office, and the mayor was there with them like he said he would be.

When the meeting started, the Chairman said that he had a question for me, and asked me if the city could resurface each church's parking lots, since all of these churches wee old, their parking lots were deteriorating, and such resurfacing would make it easier for their respective church members to park their cars when they arrived to attend the weekly services held at their respective churches.

I responded that the City could on resurface parking lots on public property, since such work was financed with money generated from those citizens that owned property in the community. I noted that the church parking lots, legally, were on private property, and that their respective congregations should pay the cost for such repaving services. I said that this was the law, and that the city had to follow it!

They did not like my response, but thanked me for attending their meeting and answering this question for them. They said that they would follow-up knowing that ach church was legally responsible for their respective church parking lots.

When the meeting was over, and all of the church folks left, and the mayor was in his office, I went to his office to talk to him. I said that you knew this answer, as I did, and why didn't you explain these requirements to them (i.e., the use of tax dollars for improvements to public vs. private property).

The mayor told me, and I learned from his response, that he knew what the answer was, but that he was elected to his office by the members of these churches, and that he would answer any positive questions that they may ask, but that he would call on me to answer any negative responses that might be required to respond to their issues and questions, which I did.

This is the difference between an elected official and a professional administrator. I told the mayor that this was my job, and that I would be happy to respond to such questions from other community groups in the future if the City's response was negative, and he wanted me to articulate the City's response to the citizens that attended such meetings.

After all, he was elected to his Office by the citizens, including all church members, and I was appointed by the City's elected officials (i.e., their Mayor and City Council members).

This is one of the major differences between elected and appointed public officials – at all levels of government!

The Headquarters of the "Hells Angels"

I once worked in a city where the Hells Angels, a highly nationally recognized motorcycle club, was recognized by virtually all of the citizens that lived in California, had their headquarters.

I was an Assistant to the City Manager, and as walking to lunch with a friend of mine one day, and we walked by their "headquarters," which was on the main street in our community.

As we were walking by their headquarters, I told the friend of mine that some of them parked their motorcycles on the street in an illegal parking area, and that I can go in their headquarters and tell them or that I can call the Chief of Police, to inform him of this illegal parking violation, and that he would send out our Police Officers to solve this problem.

My friend told me that we were both out for lunch, and that we were not working, so why should we do this? I recognized his response, and realized that we are not on our 24/7 working-time, so why should I worry about this minor municipal legal violation?

I thanked him for his response, and said that we should ignore this violation, since we were not "on duty," and that we should head-on for our lunch in our city's downtown area.

He agreed, and I agreed – and then we went to lunch and ignored the parking violation of the Hells Angels Motorcycle Club, since we should not pay attention to this violation during our off-duty lunch hour.

I recognized, at this time, that public officials do not work 24/7, but that we only work from 9:00 a.m. to 5:00 p.m. on weekdays, during our regular working hours.

And that we should all appreciate our time off, including our lunch hours!

I believe that the City's Chapter of the Hells Angels received a great deal based on these favorable municipal employee government decisions, that were made during our lunch hours.

The Hells Angels Motorcycle Club is still in existence, and they still have an excellent national reputation, and their headquarters is still located in a great City, in the State of California.

Being Stopped by the Police — Speeding

I was driving my car one morning to work, was running a little bit late, and was going a few miles per hour over the City's legal speed limit – not much, only a few miles per hour!

A Police Officer, in his car with his red-lights flashing, stopped me. He got out of his car, and walked up to the driver's window in my car and said – I am sorry that I stopped you, I did not recognize your car.

I told him that I want you to treat me like anyone else, and that I do not want any special treatment because I am the City Manager. I went on to say please honor my request.

He walked back to his car, stayed there a few minutes, then walked back to my car. He told me that I am giving you a warning not to speed again, or I will give you a ticket. He said that this is a normal response, and that I give it to a lot of citizens that I stop for speeding.

I told him "Thank You," and started my car and continued my drive on to work at City Hall.

I felt lucky, but I also was satisfied that he treated me like everyone else – a warning this time, but that I will receive a ticket the next time.

I slowed down in the future when I drove to work, even if I was going to be a little late.

Gifts from Citizens

I was driving to work one morning and, on the way, I stopped at a local donut shop, at their drive-thru window, to get a cup of coffee and a couple of donuts.

When the person in front of me left the drive-up window, I pulled-up to place my order. Before I could place my order, the donut shop employee at the window told me that the person in front of me, that just pulled out, gave her an extra $10.00, and he said that he was paying for my order in advance so that I would not have to pay anything.

So, I placed my order, and wrote down the license plate number of the car in front of me that just paid my bill, and when I got back to my office, after having my donuts and coffee, I called the Chief of Police, and gave him the vehicle license number of the car in front of me at the donut shop that paid my bill.

I told the Chief of Police that I wanted that person's mailing address, since he paid my bill at the local donut shop in their drive-thru line, and I wanted to pay him back, since I do not accept gifts from our citizens – even if they are only coffee and donuts

The Chief called back a few minutes later, and gave me the person's name and mailing address. When I got home that night, I made out a check to him for $10.00 and wrote on a note to him that I was reimbursing him for paying for my order at the donut shop the other morning. I also wrote on the note to him that I do not accept any gifts from our citizens.

This made me feel good, since I did not want any other citizens to be paying for my food orders at local donut shops, or any other local eateries, at any time.

I felt that this is how it should be done, and that I did the right thing!

LESSON FIVE

FINANCE AND BUDGETING SERVICES

Mayor's Request to Balance the Budget

I was a newly appointed City Manager, and one day the mayor walked into my office, and told me that the City Council trusted my financial judgement, and that they wanted me to look at their budget and tell them what they would have to reduce to balance it without having a tax increase.

He said that it was an election year, and the City Council did not want to raise taxes, since they would lose votes and that they might not get re-elected if they did so.

I thought about what the mayor said to me, and I responded as follows.

I told the mayor that a city's budget expenses were 75 to 80 percent salaries and fringe benefits, and this is because the highest expenses in the City's budget are to pay for our employees to provide their respective departmental services to the public.

I told the mayor that I could come up with some "nickel and dime" budget reductions, but that any major budget reductions would only result if we laid-off employees, since their respective salaries and fringe benefits were most of the City's annual budget expense.

I went on to say, Mayor to do major cuts to receive significant budget reductions, our city would have to lay-off some of its employees. I asked him what employees would he and the City Council want me to reduce – Police Officers, Fire Fighters, Public Works employees, Parks and Recreation employees, or employees that provide other City and staff services.

The mayor responded that, since it was an election year, that the City Council did not want to lay-off any City employees.

I responded that this was a good idea, so why don't I review other portions of the City's budget, not employee salaries and their fringe benefits, and I will make a list of politically acceptable budget reductions, and we could balance our city's budget without having to lay-off any of our employees.

But we would likely have a small budget increase due to inflation, and the increase in the cost of what we purchase to provide our services to the public. He said that was a good idea, and I went on to achieve this goal with our budget for the coming fiscal yar.

Later in the year the Mayor and City Council voted to approve the proposed budget with no employee lay-offs, and we had a small budget increase for the coming fiscal year!

The City Council Finance Committee

In most cities that I worked in, the City Charter noted that the City Manager prepared the City's annual budget, and then presented it to the Mayor and City Council for their consideration, and ultimate approval.

Most cities had this type of a legal arrangement with their City Budget Process. I would prepare their annual budget, working with the Finance Director, then it would be submitted to the Mayor and City Council for their consideration, and their budget process would typically take at least four or five hours to complete.

In one City that I worked in, the City's elected officials, its Mayor and City Council, had

City Council Committees for its major departments. One of their City Council Committees was called The City Council Finance Committee.

I would prepare the City's annual budget, working with the Finance Director, then I would present the City's proposed budget for the coming fiscal year to the City Council at one of their public meetings.

Since the Mayor and City Council had a City Council Finance Committee, they would forward their annual budget to them, and they would hold, usually weekly public meetings, on the City's annual budget. The entire City Council had twelve elected members.

There were five City Council members on The City Council Finance Committee, and they would hold at least one, sometimes two, public meetings each week, with the following steps in their budget review and approval process. These steps included.

- They would hold evening, sometimes Saturday meetings, several of them, to review each department's budget. At each of these meetings, the City Manager and Finance Director would be there, as well as each Department Manager that was having his/her budget reviewed.
- When this departmental budget review process was over, they would hold another session to review the revenues in the proposed Annual Budget for the coming fiscal year. Usually, the Finance Director and City Manager would attend these meetings, which were also open to the public.

When the City Council Finance Committee completed its annual budget review process, they would vote to recommend approval of the proposed budget to the Mayor and City Council at an upcoming public meeting.

So, at the final City Council meeting on the City's annual budget, it was the City Council Finance Committee making a recommendation for approval of the City's proposed budget for the coming fiscal year to the entire City Council.

I thought this was great, since at this final meeting on the budget, it was elected officials recommending approval of the budget to other elected officials. The City's budget was nearly always unanimously approved using this budget review and approval process!

The City Council Budget Approval Process

In most cities that I worked in, The City Charter noted that the City Manager prepared the City's annual budget, and then presented it to the Mayor and City Council for their consideration, and ultimate approval.

Most cities had this type of a legal arrangement with their City Budget Process. I would prepare their annual budget, working with the Finance Director, then it would be submitted to the Mayor and City Council for their consideration.

Every time I did this, the City's budget was presented to the Mayor and City Council at one of their public meetings, they would discuss the budget, and ask questions, and after they were done, usually after a couple of hours, the budget review and approval process went to the next step.

This was when the Mayor and City Council called the Public Hearing to order, and citizens were allowed to ask questions about the proposed budget, as well as questions about its revenue sources, and their property taxes. Frequently this could also take a couple of hours.

Then, after these two steps in the budget-approval process unfolded, the Mayor and City Council would hold a discussion after the citizens spoke, asked any questions any of them wished to the City Manager and Finance Director, then they would hold a vote to approve the City's budget for the coming fiscal year.

Frequently, during this budget-approval process, some minor changes would be made to departmental budgets, and some minor adjustments could be made to some of the City's revenue sources.

When this process was done, which took four to five hours, the Mayor and City Council would vote to approve the budget. While a majority vote was needed to do this, after these budget sessions, the budget approval vote was usually unanimous.

This is to show the budget approval process works in most of our nation's Cities.

Balancing a City's Annual Budget

I was a newly appointed City Manager, and the Finance Director informed me that the City was facing a financial deficit for the coming fiscal yar.

I asked the Finance Director to set-up a meeting with me and the City's Auditor. In most cities the City Auditor is a contracted-out annual service function that is performed by a private auditing company, and is a project that is usually put out-to-bid and approved by the City Council.

During this meeting the Finance Director and I learned that several of the City's General Funds has a fund balance for nearly twenty percent, which is higher than fund balances in most communities. The City Auditor agreed with this statement.

I went back to the mayor and told him that I met with the City Auditor and the Finance Director to review our General Fund's fund balances, and that several of our sources of revenues in our General Fund had annual fund balances of nearly twenty percent.

The mayor said that he and the City Council liked having a twenty percent fun balance in these General Funds, and that they wanted to keep it this way. I told him that if we did this, that the city would have to lay-off dozens of employees during the coming fiscal year to balance its annual budget. I asked the mayor to let me do some research and that I would get back with him.

I checked recommended Fund Balance requirements by national financial and accounting association, and then checked some Wall Street firms about their financial evaluation criteria, then I got back with the mayor with the results of this research.

When I next met with the Mayor, I told him that national financial and accounting professional associations though that a ten percent fund balance in a City's General Fund was great, and that the Wall Street financial evaluators also felt that this was a reasonable and respected General Fund balance. In fact, those Cities that had a ten percent General Fund balance usually got the highest, or a AAA (Triple "A") Bond Ratings.

When I talked to the mayor, he generally liked what I had to say. When I was done talking about required General Fund Balances, he said that I would review this item with the City Council and get back with me during the coming week.

When the Mayor got back with me, he told me that both he and the City Council agreed that a ten percent General Fund Balance was a reasonable, and was an acceptable fund balance, and that the City's elected officials could live with this revised General Fund balance requirement.

Hence, during the coming fiscal year, the City's staff recommended a balanced budget, by using surplus General Fund balances, and that we left the General Fund balance at ten percent, and that we did not have to lay-off any city employees during the coming fiscal year to balance our budget.

Everyone, the Mayor and City Council, the City Manager and the Finance Director, and the City's management staff, all agreed with their decision and no employees had to be laid-off!

Possible Budget Reductions

At a Department Manager Meeting, which I would usually hold once a month, one of the items on the agenda was to talk about possible ways to reduce the City's budget for the coming fiscal year since we were facing a financial deficit.

Several department managers were talking about possible ways to save funds, and to balance our budget, so that we would not have to lay-off any of our city's employees during the coming fiscal year. This discussion included several possible budget reduction options.

One was from the newly appointed Fire Chief, who said that it looked like we had one to many fire stations, and that we could close one of them without having a major impact on our city's fire services. He was the newly appointed Fire Chief, and he reviewed all of our fire stations, and he thought that we could close one of them.

This possible budget reduction option, after it was presented, was being talked about all around our City Hall, and this possible budget reduction for the coming fiscal year was even known and discussed informally by our City's Mayor and City Council.

A few days later, the mayor came to me and told me that the City Council does not want to close any of the City's fire stations. He told me to exclude this budget reduction option from the City's budget for the coming fiscal year.

I told the mayor that I would do this! After all, I'm appointed by the City's Mayor and City Council and they want me to do what they wish by their majority vote. This was one of the budget reduction options that they did not want me to pursue for the coming fiscal year.

So, I would meet with the City's department managers during the coming months and look at other ways to balance the City's budget for the coming fiscal yar, but closing a fire station was not one of the options that was under consideration.

The Mayor and City Council voted on a proposed budget for the coming fiscal year, and it did not include any options that involved closing any City fire station.

After all, the citizens vote for their elected representatives, and I follow their recommendations by majority vote, since this is one of my most important job requirements.

After all, I am appointed to my job by the City's Mayor and City Council by their majority vote!

Compare Your City's Property Tax Rate

In one City that I was a City Manager in, some City Council members came to me asking me about our City's Property Tax Rate, and how does it compare to other cities within our County?

I thought about this, and then prepared a listing of all of the cities in our County, including the following information.

- Each City's Name,
- Each City's Population, and
- Each City's Property Tax Rate.

I did this for all of the cities in our County, and all of this information was public information so I only had to collect it, and place all of this information on a one-sheet flier.

I gave copies to our Mayor and City Council, to all of our Department Managers, and also made them available in the Office of the Mayor, Office of the City Manager, and our Public Library, for all of our citizens to take a copy and review this information.

I even gave a copy to our local media people, that worked at our local newspapers and our local television stations.

This information revealed that our city was among the largest in our County, and that our Property Tax Rate was among the lowest in our County.

This made our city look good, since we had a fairly large population, provided typical public services, and had a fairly low property tax rate.

The Mayor and City Council liked this information, and they also helped me distribute this Property Tax Rate flier to the citizens thorough out our city!

Citizen Budget Request

The city that I was a City Manager in, had a chapter of a national senior citizens association, and they would hold monthly meetings in the conference room of a local non-profit organization. At one of their meetings, I was asked to be their Guest Speaker. They wanted me to fill about an hour of time, which I did.

I talked about the city, its budget and operations, and at the end of my presentation some of their members asked me some questions.

When I was done with the City Manager's presentation at their meeting, there were a few great questions, that I will highlight below, including my response to it.

One female senior citizen, a resident of the city, said that the City's budget goes up every year, even when no new public services are added to it. Why?

After some quick introspective reflection, I responded to this lady's question as follows. Mam, the City's annual budget includes items that we buy every year, like police vehicles, computers, paper and ink, gasoline, and hundreds of other small items, like paper, printer ink, computer maintenance, and the like. These items are just our normal annual operating expenses. We have no control over their costs.

For all of these items that we purchase, their price usually goes up annually! Just like everything else that citizens, and City's buy, during the year!

For example, if you go to your local market a year later to buy the same thing that you did last year, what happens? You know that all of the items that you usually purchase have increased in their respective costs and frequently even the quantity of these items gets smaller. So sometimes the cost of what you buy increases, and sometimes even the quantity of the product that you buy gets smaller in size.

These trends are built into our economy – the price of the items that you purchase every year at your store increases, and frequently the quantity of the items that you get for this price decreases.

Everything that the city purchases annually, like what you purchase at your local grocery store, goes up in price, and sometimes the quantity down in size – every year.

We don't like these annual increases to our city's budget any more than you do in your personal budget. We don't like paying these cost increases any more than you do. But we have to, like you, since we have no choice.

She thanked me for my comments, and told me that she agreed with me!

Union Labor Contracts

In one City, where I was appointed as their new City Manager, the City Council wanted me to do some labor relations things with different City employee unions, but I could not since they were against the existing City-Union Labor Agreements that were approved by the previous City Council.

I went to the City Attorney, and he explained that the previous City Council, which was more liberal, approved these labor agreements with the City's Labor Unions, and that all of these contracts were approved by them, many of whom were not reelected during the last City election.

Now the new City Council, which is more conservative than the previous one, wanted me to do some labor-related things that were against the current Employee City – Union Labor Agreements.

I went to the City Attorney, and he told me that I could go to the City's Union Presidents and asked them if they would like to re-open labor negotiations, which would have to be approve by them and a vote of their respective employees. I told him that I would do this!

So, I called all of the Union Presidents together for a meeting with me in my office. I explained that the current City Council wanted me to make some changes to their current City – Union Labor Agreements, and that I needed them to vote to reopen negotiation with the City to do this.

They knew that the previous City Council was more liberal in nature, that the current newly-elected City Council was more conservative, and that they were trying to reduce labor costs to save the City's taxpayers some money during the coming fiscal year.

These Union Presidents, collectively, told me "No," they did not want to do this, since the current City Council would change things that they would not like changed. This was also the law, since the current City – Union Labor Agreements were unanimously approved by the City's previous City Council.

I went back to the City Council to tell them this, and they blamed me for not being able to re-open union negotiations with them to help achieve the newly-elected City Council's financial goals for the coming fiscal year.

I was the new City Manager appointed by the new City Council but, legally, I had to follow the City's labor agreements that were approved by the previous City Council, the liberal ones that no longer held public office in this City.

Together, the new City Council and I, their new City Manager, worked on other ways to reduce the City's labor costs during the coming fiscal year.

Some of the did not like me, but I was only following the law – and I was doing what I legally, and professionally, had to do. This process is required for a City Manager to be a professional.

Departmental Programs and User Fees

A newly-elected City Council member once told me that he would like our city government to operate like the private sector. That is, our departmental program user fees should make a program cost-covering from a review standpoint.

I asked him specifically what his concern was, and he said that we charge children $1.00 to go swimming in our public municipal swimming pool. He asked if the current user fee made this program cost-covering? I told him that I would check this out and get back with him.

Then I met with the Finance Director, and he determined that the current charge of $1.00 per person generated 20 percent of the annual operating cost of our city's municipal swimming pool.

So, to make the fee for this service cost-covering, the city would have to charge $5.00 per person, which would be 500 percent increase in this departmental user fee (i.e., $100 to $5.00 per person).

I went back to the City Council member that asked this question and explained tis to him. I also went on to say that to make this City service cost-covering that we would have to raise the user fee to $5.00 per person. This could never happen, since young people, and their parents, could not afford to pay a user fee to use our pool at this level.

I went on to tell the city council member that government is not like the private sector, and that some services are not, and will never be, cost-covering. For example, our municipal library checks out books for free, and citizens only pay a small charge if they are late when they are returned. This has been the case forever relative to a library's public services.

I also said that there are certain services that are very expensive, that citizens do not pay directly for – like police and fire services. These services are paid for through a citizen's property taxes, and not by any user fee charges that are imposed by the City on citizens using the services of these departments.

He listened to me, and finally agreed, that government is different than the private sector – it has been in the past and always will be in the future!

He thanked me for checking this out, and said he was learning more-and-more about local governments as a newly elected official.

Personal Property Taxes

Many state laws permit their cities to assess the value of their citizens real property and personal property for their business. This would not include the property taxes on a person's home in the city that they live in.

Citizens that own a business in a city must register their personal property and real property, which is assessed, and then the city applies their annual tax rate to this value to determine the amount of taxes that a business owner must pay annually to their city.

Real property includes the value of the land and its improvements, while personal property includes the value of medical and dental equipment, business machines, computers, copiers, and related business equipment.

Since some business person were not properly recording all of their personal property, a city could hire a private assessment company to come into their city, review businesses, and make sure that they were reporting all of their personal property, had the right value on it, and were paying annual personal property taxes on it, as required by their state law.

When an outside consultant stated to do this, many business owners got mad, and called their local city business association and their representatives were calling me up asking me why the city was doing this, since it was forcing business owners to pay more personal property taxes on items that they had not previously registered with their city, and they were not paying the appropriate taxes one.

I told these people that this requirement was a State and City law, and that business owners had to report their personal property, and make sure that it had the right value on it, so that they were paying the appropriate personal property taxes on it.

After all, this was the law, in both their State and City governments!

I told anyone that contacted me about this that the City was only following the law, and that business owners were required by law to report all personal property that was located at their respective businesses. In this case the city was merely making sure that that were following the law.

The bottom-line was that their city was only making then follow the State and City laws in regard to this legal personal property registration and payment requirements!

Contracting Out Public Services

In one city, as their new City Manager, the city faced a budget deficit for the coming fiscal year, and the City Council wanted me to do whatever I could to save money that would help balance the City's budget for the coming fiscal year.

Some City Council members even mentioned the possibility of contracting-out some public services if it would be cheaper for the private sector to provide selected services to the city.

I reviewed the City's departmental services, and their respective budgets, and came up with a list of selected services that the City might be able to contract-out to the private sector.

If the City did a Request for Proposal (RFP) for each of these services, and we placed them out to bid to private sector companies, we would find out immediately if we could help save funds to balance the City's budget for the coming fiscal year.

This would also help avoid the need to lay-off any City employees to balance the City's budget for the coming fiscal year.

Once I made up a list of these services to possibly contract out for, I went to the City Attorney to find out if it was legal for the City to contract out these municipal public services.

The City Attorney looked at this list of public services, all of which were currently provided by City employees, then went on to check the City–Union Contracts with each of these Employee Unions. Such contracts are approved by a vote of respective Employee Union members, then they are approved by the City Council.

Every Union Contract contained a phrase that it was against the law to contract out any service to the private sector that was proved by their respective employees. The City Attorney, after checking the Union Contracts, said that I could not legally contract out any of these services.

I went back to the City Council and explained this to them, and they agreed that I had no choice and that I could not contract out any of the services that are provided by the employees of City's Employee Unions.

I looked for other revenue sources, other service reductions, and had department heads work with me to also reduce our budget costs. After all of this the City still had a financial deficit for the coming fiscal year.

I then met with the City's Union Presidents, and we had a meeting on how to balance the City's budget without have to lay-off any City employees. My goal was to avoid having to lay-off any City employees. The Union Presidents liked this idea!

All of the Union Presidents, and their respective union members, agreed, and the City Council approved, a work furlough program where everyone would take one-week off work during the next fiscal year, and this would balance the City's budget without having to lay-off any of its employees.

Funds for the Homeless Shelter

One year, during a City's Annual Budget Process, a City Council member came to me and said that he did not like funding the City's Homeless Shelter, which was operated by a local non-profit organization.

He was a new City Council member, and he said that our Homeless Shelter might be attracting homeless people from other neighboring communities, and he did not like that. He also said that some other cities in our area do not have Homeless Shelters.

I told this City Council member that I would do some research on the issues that e presented, and that I would get back to him within the week, and he said that was fine and he was glad that I would be checking into these possible problems for him.

On night that week, I personally went to the Homeless Shelter to see who was staying there, and where they were from. I also talked to the Director of the Homeless Shelter about these issues.

When I saw the City Council member about a week later, I told him that I went to the

Homeless Shelter, talked to its director, and wanted to relate the following facts that I found out during this process. These facts were:

– There were twenty-one folks at the Homeless Shelter,
– Only two of them were minority folks,
– All were citizens of our community,
– Not one person was from any out-of-town community, and
– Most were older people with drug and/or alcohol problems

After I told him these facts, I mentioned that if these individuals could not stay at the Homeless Shelter, that they would probably be staying public areas in our downtown.

The City Council member thanked me for my research on these Homeless Shelter issues, and said that he would vote to fund the Homeless Shelter for the coming fiscal year.

This City Council member was pleased to receive these facts, and I was happy to do the necessary research that had to be done to present them to him.

We both also explained these facts about the City's Homeless Shelter to the Mayor and other members of the City Council.

The City's Mayor and City Council voted unanimously to approve funds for "our" Homeless Shelter for the coming year!

City With a Municipal Marina

This City that I was working at was facing a deficit for the coming fiscal year, and I talked to the mayor about his, and he told me to look for ways to save money and to present some options to him, and that he would present the to the City Council for their consideration.

Certain City services should be treated as an Enterprise Fund, the public-sector word for a service that should be treated like a profit center. Citizens that do not use such a service should not have to pay for it, like for boat mooring fees at a City Marina.

I told the mayor that the mooring fees that boat owners paid to the city generated about 75 percent of the annual operating costs of this municipal facility, and they should be increased to make this service cost-covering.

After all, citizens that did not own boats should not be paying to operate such a facility, since it should be cost-covering, and that only the users of this type of a service should have to pay for it. The citizens that have boats and use this facility should pay 100 percent of its annual operating cost.

This was a logical financial viewpoint, and I mentioned this to the mayor, and he did not like the idea, stating that he and the City Council would not want to increase citizen boat mooring fees for their respective boats at our City Marina.

While I personally did not agree with this philosophy, when I thought about it, I felt that citizens that owned boats were wealthier than other citizens, and that possibly any of them knew our elected officials, and that they possibly even donated funds to them at election time. This seemed like a logical viewpoint from a political standpoint.

So, I respected the mayor's viewpoint, and sought out other possible ways for the City to save funds during the coming fiscal year to balance its budget. Also, I am an administrator, and not a politician, and I felt that I mut respect the mayor's viewpoint on this issue.

City With a Public Golf Course

The City that I was working in was facing a financial deficit for the coming fiscal year, and I talked to the City Council about this, and they told me to look for ways to save money and to present some options to him for their consideration.

Certain City services should be treated as an Enterprise Fund. The public sector financial word for public service that should be treated like a profit center. Citizens that do not use such a service should not have to pay for it, like playing golf at a City Golf Course.

I told the City Council that the golf course fees paid by citizens to play golf at our City Golf Course generated about two-thirds of the annual operating costs of our City Golf Course. I also mentioned that this fee should be increased by one-third to make this service totally cost-covering.

After all, citizens that do not play golf should not be paying to operate such a public facility, since it should be cost-covered City service. This service fee should be increased to make it cost-covering so the citizens that use it pay for it, and pay 100 percent of its annual operating costs.

I went to the mayor and explained this to him, and he asked me who primarily plays golf on the City's Golf Course. I told him that it looked like mostly senior citizens played golf at our City Golf course.

He agreed, and then he said what group of citizens are our primary voters at election time? I said that it seems like mostly senior citizens vote at election time. H said that I was right, and that this was an election year, and that I should come back to the City Council next year with this financial recommendation.

I came back to them a yar later, and the City Council unanimously approved an increase in our city golf fees to make this service 100 percent cost-covering

Since I am not a politician, I did not think that I was asking them to increase our golf course fees during an election year. Some of the elected officials felt that they might not get re-elected if they did this.

So, I waited a year, and the City Council approved it! This is a national trend to make this public service cost-covering from a user fee perspective. Non-users should not have to pay for it!

LESSON SIX

POLICE AND FIRE SERVICES

The Chief of Police Appointment Process

In one City that I worked in the Chief of Police had retired, and I appointed the Deputy Chief of Police to be the Acting Chief of Police. This was a common practice I would follow if a department was large enough to have an Assistant Director, I would appoint him/her to be the Acting Department Manager.

I would usually keep the Acting Department Manager in this position for six months to determine how he/she performed. If they did a good job, and everyone was pleased, both the elected officials as well as the department's employees, I would make the Acting Department Manager the Permanent Department Manager.

When the Acting Chief of Police was appointed, I received several enquiries from City Council members not to make him/her the Permanent Department Manager, since he/she did not live in our town. He/she lived in a neighboring community.

It was not a City Charter requirement that the Chief of Police had to live in our city. The only city employee that was legally required to live in the city was the City Manager.

After a few months, I, along with others, thought that the Acting Chief of Police was doing an excellent job. After all, he worked his way up through the department over many years, and had an excellent knowledge of the department, its employees, and its operations.

I explained to the City Council, that legally the Chief of Police did not have to live in our city only the City Manager did. I also explained to them that he lived only a few miles from our City Hall, even though he lived in a neighboring city. He could drive to work quicker than most employees that lived in the city could.

Also, he and his wife had three children in high school in the neighboring community where they lived, and it would not be appropriate to require the Chief of Police to place his children in a different high school, since it would serve no purpose.

When I wanted to make him the Permanent Chief of Police, I informed the City Council of my plan to appoint him to this position, and not require him to move to our city to accept this position, since it was legally not required.

At this time, the Mayor and City Council agreed with me, the Acting Chief of Police was doing a great job, and I subsequently appointed him as our Permanent Chief of Police. He held this position for many years after his appointment.

The Chief of Police And The Police Commission

In almost every City that I worked in, the City Manager was responsible for appointing all department managers, including the Chief of Police.

In a couple of cities that I worked in one City Council had a Public Safety Committee, and another City had a City Police Commission.

The City Council reviewed all agenda items, and referred those items related to the Police and Fire Departments to their Public Safety Committee for their review, discussion, and recommendation back to the full City Council for their final vote.

In the other City that I worked, the City's Charter had a Police Commission, which consisted of members who ran for this position and were elected by the citizens. The Police Commission held monthly meetings, and approved any changes or additions to the Police Department's budget and operations.

This City's Police Commission was also responsible for hiring the City's Chief of Police, and they also had the legal responsibility to terminate his/her employment if they wished.

One day the Chief of Police came to see me, and said that he did not like working for a Police Commission, since some of the members of it were former Police Officers, and they were high school graduates, who served on this Commission, and they were his boss.

He also said that, while he does not live in the city, he does not like having citizens serve on the Police Commission that were formerly Police Officers and were only high school graduates, since he had a master's degree in his field, and did not like having high school graduates as his boss.

I agreed with the Chief of Police, and when I departed a few years later, he was still there, so I guess that he learned how to work with the members of the City's Police Commission, and if you like what they do, you will stay there for a long time.

The Chief of Police also said that my job is like yours! You are hired and fired by the City's Mayor and City Council, and I am hired and fired by the City's Police Commission.

Charges Against the Chief of Police

I was a newly appointed City Manager, and within my first week in office, the mayor came to my office to talk to me about the City's Chief of Police. He said that he should be terminated for the following reasons:

— Employee morale in the Police Department is very low,
— Police Officer turn-over in our Police Department is very high,
— Our Police Department does not use state-of-the-art technology, and
— The Police Department's Employee Union would also like him fired for these reasons.

I wrote these items down, and told the mayor that I would like to check these complaints out, and that I would get back to him. The next day the President of the Police Department Employee Union came to my office to see me, and he said the same thing.

The City's Police Department Union paid for a large half-page ad in a respected local newspaper, noting the items that the mayor told me about, and this paid-for advertisement also noted that the City Manager should fire the Chief of Police.

I thought about these demands on me and, since I was a new City Manager that I should make an appointment with the most seasoned City Manager in our County, and inform him of these demands that were being placed on me by my City's Mayor and the President of our Police Department Employee Union.

I met with him, and he said that what he would do, if he was me, would be as follows:

– Our state government has a Police Commission, and they have some full-time Police Consultants that work for them, and that they were all retired Chiefs of Police

– He suggested that I call them and submit a request to them for a Management Consulting Study of my City's Police Department to determine if these allegations were true and, if they were, what was causing them, and what actions I should take to solve them.

– He told me that when I received the State Police Commission Consulting Proposal, and how much such a study would cost, that I should present it to my City Council for their review and approval.

– He also said that when I got the consulting proposal, and knew how much it cost, that I should contact the Mayor and the President of my Police Department Employee Union, and thank them for bringing these items to my attention, and that I wanted to have this study done to find out the facts, and then I would take the appropriate action.

The City Council unanimously approved the State Police Commission Study Proposal, and they also allocated funds from the City's budget to pay for it.

A few weeks later, two Police Consultants, from the State Police Commission, who were both retired Chiefs of Police, came to our city for several days to conduct this study. They also checked on the status of these allegations made against our Chief of Police with other neighboring Police Departments. When their research was done, they returned to their home office, and prepared a draft of their study on my City's Police Department, and they had me review it before it was finalized.

When they came to my office to review the draft of their consulting study on my City's Police Department, they related the following information:

– Moral in my City's Police Department was low because the City Council wanted the Chief of Police to reduce our Police Department's budget expenses, therefore the Chief of Police reduced the overtime expenses paid to our Police Officers. The City Council wanted this done since the city was facing a budget deficit for the coming fiscal year.

– The turn-over rate in my City's Police Department was normal when compared with the turn-over rate in the Police Departments of neighboring communities in our area.

– The technologies that were used in our Police Department were similar to the types of police technologies that were being used in other Police Departments in neighboring communities in our area.

– The Police Department Employee Union wanted the Chief of Police to be terminated because he reduced the overtime payments of our City's Police Officers, and that they did not like this, so many of them went to their union for follow-up action, like terminating our City's Chief of Police for this reason.

This study was presented to the City Council, they received and discussed it, and they all agreed with the findings in the study since it was done by the State Police Commissions Consultants, who were independent from us, politically neutral, and the study was conducted by retired Chiefs of Police.

I went on to tell the mayor that I had to follow these findings and, had they been otherwise, I would have terminated our Chief of Police, but that I could not do so based on the independent, politically neutral, findings of this study on our City's Police Department by the State Police Commission.

I felt that I did the right thing, everything quieted down once this study was done, and the Chief of Police had a solid position with the City for many years to come!

When I left this City for another City Manager job a few years later, the Chief of Police was still there. I later heard that he retired several years later at the end of his career as the Chief of Police!

Our City's Murder Rate

In one city, when I was younger, I was an Assistant to the City Manager, and worked in the Office of the City Manager. The City Manager assigned some departments for me to work with, one of which was our Police Department. To do this, I worked on police issues with the Chief of Police and his management staff.

One day the local regional newspaper had a front-page article noting that our city was the Murder Capitol of the West Coast. The newspaper noted that we had more murders annually in our city than any other City in our state.

Once I read this article, I went to see the Chief of Police, and asked him why our city was the Murder Capitol of the West Coast. He said to me that he knew this, and that he was proud of it. I asked him why he was proud of it, and he said that the murders in our city usually consist of one drug deal shooting another over a drug-sale territorial dispute.

The Chief said that the more drug dealers that kill each other the better, since it makes our community safe for our citizens, and it reduces the sale of illegal drugs to drug users in our city.

Once he told me this, it seemed to make sense, and I agreed with him

I tried to call the newspaper to explain this to them, but the newspapers like to write about the bad news not the good news. Hence, they only wrote articles about our city being the Murder Capitol of the West Coast, not on why there were so many murders.

So, when future articles of this nature appeared in our local regional newspaper, I never contacted the Chief of Police again. Also, when I was asked to speak to community groups about the City's services, I would explain why we were the Murder Capitol of the West Coast.

Most citizens agreed with me once I told them that our murder rate was primarily based on one drug dealer shooting another over a drug dealer territorial dispute.

Request from the Chief of Police

It was a typical Monday morning, and I just arrived in the Office of the City Manager, and sat down at my desk, to start my work week.

The Chief of Police walks into my office to inform me that we must arrest a City Council member, since he was seen by one of our Police Officers smoking marijuana over the weekend.

I asked the Chief to explain the details, and he said that someone over the weekend call the Police Department and wanted a Police Officer to go to a house that was holding a party, and some of the neighbors thought that it was too late at night, and that they were creating too much noise.

The Police Officer went to this location, looked around, told them to quiet it down, and he saw one of our City Council members smoking marijuana.

I told the Chief to let me talk to the City Attorney, and that I would get back with him shortly. When I related this to the City Attorney, he said that we needed answers to three questions:

- How many people were at the party?
- How many people were smoking marijuana?
- How many people were arrested for smoking marijuana?

I called the Chief and told him that I needed answers to these three questions. H talked with the Police Officer that responded to this "loud noise" incident, and the Chief came to my office to answer these questions for me.

The Chief of Police said that there were about a dozen people at the party, and that most of them were smoking marijuana, and that no one was arrested. I told the Chief that I would check with our City Attorney and get back with him later today.

I checked with the City Attorney, and told him the answers to these three questions he had asked. What the City Attorney said was that if we only arrested one person, why – because he is a City Council member? He also said that if the city did this that we would have a lawsuit filed against us for a lot of money, and that we would certainly lose this case, since a lot of citizens were guilty and no one else was arrested.

The City Attorney and I agreed, and I told the Chief that when something like this happens again tell your Police Officers to arrest everyone that is breaking the law, not just one person because she/he is related to the city.

I felt that everyone did the right thing, and that if something like this ever happened again that the Police Officers involved would arrest everyone that had broken the law. This would be the right thing to do, and avoid lawsuits against the City for Police Officers not doing the right thing!

Police Services in a Wealthy City

I was invited to go through a job interview for a City's City Manager Recruitment Process. I was honored since it was a very wealthy community, with few financial and operational issues and problems.

When I was going through the interview process, the Mayor and City Council informed me that they have a low-crime community, and they want to their Police Officers to promote this achievement.

They said that their city's Police Officer Patrols, in their police cars, usually take place with their Police Officers driving their police cars through alleys, on back roads in outlaying neighborhoods with few Police Officers driving their police cars on the Main Street in their downtown areas.

Since this City's citizens knew that their city had a low-crime rate, the Mayor and City Council did not want to alter this viewpoint by having their Police Officers drive their police cars on the Main Street, and other major roadways, in their city.

I did not ask them, but I would assume that if someone called 911, that the Police Officer responding to this call would respond promptly, even if it included driving on their Main Street to get to the crime scene.

After all, Police Officer response times should be prompt, and citizens would expect them to respond quickly to a crime scene for obvious reasons.

While this seemed strange, and I had never seen it before, the Mayor and City Council could approve such a Police Patrol Plan Policy by majority vote and the City Manager and Police Chief would have to implement and follow it.

Even if the Police chief did not like it, the city Manager would have to enforce what the City's elected officials, their Mayor and City Council, wanted from a police response standpoint, and the Chief of Police would have to follow this police patrolling process.

I did not get this job, and was glad, since I did not want to be responsible for enforcing such a Police Patrol Policy. I always leave this responsibility up to the City's Chief of Police.

Police Officers and Local Politics

Several years ago, when I was a City Manager in a City, a citizen called me in my office and told me that one of our City's Police Officers knocked on his door, at his home, and when he opened the door, he noticed that it was one of our Police Officers, and wanted to relate the following to me.

He asked him to vote for a few candidates that were running for City Council seats, and asked him if he was going to do so? The citizen told me that he told our Police Officer that he had not made up his mind yet as to who he was going to vote for, but thanked him for his recommendations.

The Police Officer left his front-door, and started to walk down the street to knock on the front doors of the homes of other citizens, so he could recommend who they should vote for during the upcoming City Council election.

The citizen then called me, and said that he thought that it was against the law for Police Officers to knock on doors and ask citizens to vote for certain candidates that were running for seats on our City Council.

I thanked this citizen for this information, and told him that I would check with our City Attorney, to see if this Police Officer violated rules or regulations that govern the activities of our City's Police Officers, and that I would get back to him.

Our City Attorney related the following information to me:

- Our Police Officers can take time-off, like vacation time, or do this on weekends if they were not scheduled to work.
- They only do such political things "on their own time," and not the City's time.
- He also said that they must not be wearing their Police Uniform, but could only be doing this as a citizen, on their own time.
- The city Attorney went on to state that this was legal under the above guidelines!

When I checked on this complaint, I found out that the Police Officer was not in uniform, but wearing off-duty clothing, and that he officially took time-off of work to do this, and that it was legal for him to do this for these reasons.

I called the citizen back, and informed him about this, and thanked him for telling me about this situation. I also said that it is my job to make sure that our employees follow State and City guidelines, and this employee was.

I also added that if this ever happens again, feel free to call me, since I want to make sure all of our employees are following their respective guidelines for doing such off-duty political endorsements!

Tour of City by Police Officer

As a new City Manager, I had the Chief of Police make arrangements for a Police Officer to take me on a tour of the City's downtown area.

On day I got in the Police Officer's car, and he drove me around the City's downtown area to show me high and low crim areas.

In one of the high crime areas, he was driving me through, he would point to people either walking down the street, or standing on a corner, and say the following:

- He's a drug dealers,
- She's a prostitute,
- He is a homeless person,
- He was just released from prison, and
- He went on-and-on about the people he saw on the street.

When my Police tour was over, I was well aware of the types of people that lived in portions of our downtown areas.

I am glad that I did not remember any of these people, or any of the bad things about them, since when the average citizen walks or drives their car down the street, they do not know what the Police Officer told me about some of these people that they see walking around.

For the average citizen, they should only see other citizens walking around downtown, and report any violations of the law that they see to their respective Police Departments.

Police Walking Patrols

In one City that I was a City Manager in, the downtown areas of the city had a lot of vacant stores, even office buildings, and few citizens walked around in our downtown area.

Many years earlier, a new regional shopping mall was built in the city a few miles away from the downtown are. Hence, over the years, more and more citizens drove to and did their shopping, at the shopping mall.

When I was appointed City Manager, the Mayor and City Council wanted to get more citizens to go downtown, and try to fill some of the vacant stores and office buildings in our downtown area.

I met with our Economic Development Committee, and representatives of the City's Chamber of Commerce, and we all talked about how to reinvigorate our downtown area. There was a general agreement that we should have Police Walking Patrols in our downtown area, and that this would help solve the problem.

I met with the Chief of Police, and he came up with how many Police Officers we would need, and how much it would cost. I then went back to the City Council, and they approved hiring some more Police Officers so that we could have some Downtown Walking Patrols.

While this did not solve these problems immediately, it did help over time to make citizens feel safer in our downtown area.

There was also a large influx of certain minority groups, primarily new citizens from areas South-of-the-Border. Over time, the old Polish and Italian eateries left, and new South-o-the-Border eateries started to emerge.

Nowadays, there are restaurants, cafes, a bakery, and other minority-owned businesses, with many more minority, and other citizens, going downtown then there had been in previous years.

America's cities, especially their inner-city areas, change over time, and this is what is taking place in this community! Also, the economic development effort goes on to continue the ongoing effort to fill vacant stores and offices in the downtown area.

Walking in Our Downtown

In one City that I was their City Manager, they had an aging downtown, and I was working hard with our Economic Development Director and the Planning Director to help revitalize it.

There were many old buildings, and many had a lot of vacant spaces in them. We got the Mayor and City Council to approve improvements to the streets, and their sidewalks, in the downtown are. We were also making an effort to bring non-profit organizations to our downtown to help fill vacancies and to revitalize it.

We also worked hard to bring small businesses, like cafes, pizza shops, bakeries, and other family-owned small businesses, to our Main Street. This was also going well and more vacant store spaces had been filled in recent years. This was also an ongoing economic development effort.

This was part of the City's ongoing effort to improve and revitalize its downtown. Everyone seemed to be proud of our efforts in recent years the City's elected officials, the City's staff, and the citizens.

I would walk in our downtown area several days and nights each week. This was a form of personal exercise, and also to see how things were going in our downtown area on an ongoing basis. It also helped me to get to know some of the owners of the new businesses that were locating in our downtown area.

One day when I was walking around, on a weekend, one of the City's Police Officers stopped his car next to me, and said that I should not be walking in our downtown area, since it was not safe, and that it had some crime problems. I thanked him for telling me, and then he drove away.

Monday, when I got back to work, I checked with the Chief of Police and told him what happened, and I gave him this Police Officer's name. The Chief of Police told me that this Police Officer did not live in our city, and that he would tell him not to say this anymore, since our downtown area had been improved greatly during the past few years.

This made me feel good, and it was the truth, since in my few years of walking around in our downtown area, I was only stopped once by someone that was trying to borrow some money. This, in my opinion, would not mean that our city's downtown streets were "high crime" area!

A Police Officer Called

One day, while at work in City Hall, my secretary said "a Police Officer called me, and he is waiting on the telephone to talk to you."

I picked up the telephone, and the Police Officer said that he stopped someone for speeding, and that he was going to issue them a ticket.

When he was writing the ticket, the person in the car said that they were a personal friend of the City Manager, and that he would not like the Police Officer to issue him a ticket.

The person about to receive the speeding ticket was the owner of a restaurant downtown, and it was a place where I ate lunch at now and then.

I told the Police Officer to treat this person like anyone else, and to issue him a speeding ticket since he violated the speed limit law. I also told him that if anyone ever told him not to issue them a ticket because they were the City Manager's friend, to simply ignore all such requests.

Everyone should be treated equally, even if they are a friend of elected or appointed officials that work in their city.

In all of the cities that I was a City Manager in, this was the common practice for Police Officers – to treat all citizens equally, and to issue them a ticket as is appropriate.

I was proud of such a police policy and always followed it during my City Manager career!

Being Stopped by the Police — Red Light

I was a new Interim City Manager, and one Friday night after work I was driving to a local Chamber of Commerce "mixer event" – a periodic social event that they held that would help business people get to know each other.

I had to work overtime that day, so when I was driving to this Chamber of Commerce event,

I was running late. As a matter of fact, if I did not get their quickly, it would be almost over when I got there.

I was driving down a road with a turn-lane that had a traffic signal. The light was red, but there was no traffic in sight, since it was late in the evening, and most citizens had already gone home from work.

When I stopped at this red light, to turn into the location where this event was being held, there were no cars coming down the roadway in either direction. So even though the traffic signal was red, I went on to turn into the location where this event was being held.

Then a Police Car was behind me with its red lights flashing, so I stopped my car and waited for the Police Officer to come to my car.

He came to my car, and told me that I had gone through a red light, and that he was issuing me a traffic ticket for this violation. He gave the ticket to me, and I thanked him for it.

That night, after I went home, I wrote a check out to pay for the ticket, and then I sent it on to the Police Department to pay for it.

The next Monday, when I arrived at the Office of the City Manager at City Hall, the Chief of Police came up to greet me, and he said that he heard that I received a ticket from one of his Police Officers, and that he was sorry because the Police Office did not recognize my car – since I was a newly appointed Interim City Manager.

He wanted me to give my ticket to him, and he said that he would "take care of it" for me!

I thanked the Chief of Police for his concern, and told him that I wrote a check out the same night that I received this ticket, and that I already sent it on to the Police Department to cover the cost of this violation.

I told him that I never want my tickets to be "fixed" since such actions could easily wind up on the "front page" of our local newspaper. I told him that I'd rather pay mt tickets, rather than have them "fixed" because I am the City Manager.

I thanked the Chief of Police for his offer, and then he went back to his office, and I went back to mine – and we both went back to work!

Fire Fighters and Local Politics

When I was a City Manager in a City on the East Coast, a citizen called me one day in my office and said that a few of our Fire Fighters (called Firemen in the olden days) were violating the law by doing the following:

- They had a City Fire Truck on a vacant lot in our city,
- They were all dressed in their uniforms, and
- They were all carrying political signs that encouraged our citizens to vote for certain individual candidates that were running for our City Council

I thanked this citizen for telling me this, and then I got in my city car and drove to this vacant lot to check out these complaints. What I saw on this vacant lot was as follows:

- This was an old Fire Truck, but not one used by our city,
- The off-duty Fire Fighters were wearing sweat-shirts and pants, but they were not dressed official Fire Fighter Uniforms, and
- The land that they were on was a vacant lot owned by one of our City's Fire Fighters.

When I got back to my office I called the Fire Chief, and checked with him about this citizen's complaints. The Fire Chief related the following information:

- The Fire Truck on this property was an old one that was used in City parades, and belonged to a Volunteer Fire Department in a neighboring community.
- He said that it was not one of our City's Fire Trucks.
- That all of these Fire Fighters were off-duty and on their own time.
- He also said that none of these Fire Fighters were wearing their official uniforms, but merely wearing sweat-shirts and pants that made it look like they "were-in-uniform" to the average person.

I then called back the citizen that made this complaint, and explained this situation to him, and thanked him for telling me about this situation. I also told him that it was my job to make sure that our employees follow State and City guidelines, and that these employees were. I also mentioned that all of our Fire Fighters that were on this site holding political signs were on their own-time, that they were on private property, and that none of them were on the City's time.

I added that, if this ever happens again, feel free to call me, since I want to make sure that all of our city employees are following their respective guidelines for doing such off-duty political endorsements!

Closing a Fire Station

The City I was working in was facing a financial deficit for the coming fiscal year, and all department managers were asked to think about ways for the City to save money, and to balance its budget, without having to lay-off any of our employees.

The Fire Chief came to me and said that the city had built several fire stations over the years, and that the oldest one, was a little more than a mile away from another fire station that was built later. He suggested that we close the oldest Fire Station, since it would only take a few minutes longer for a fire truck to arrive at the neighborhoods location around the old Fire Station.

This Fire Station closure was placed in the City's budget, and presented to the City Council for its consideration. Copies of the proposed budget also went to all department managers, and the union presidents.

The possible closure of this Fire Station also appeared on the front page of the local newspaper, which brought its possible closure to every ones attention, including the citizens that lived around this Fire Station.

The employee union for the Fire Fighters did some calculations, and it was determined that if their Fire Station was closed that it would take a fire truck a couple of minutes longer to get to houses in those neighborhoods that are located around the old Fire Station.

The union's employees also did some calculations to show the impact of this longer travel time, and how much more a fire would spread due to the longer fire truck response time.

They also noted that if they were responding to a health emergency, that a person could get much sicker if they did not arrive promptly, because of the longer travel time to a house located around the old Fire Station.

The night of the budget meeting, the room was full of citizens that lived around the old Fire Station. They were talking to the City Council, their elected officials, and all of them said that they did not want "their" Fire Station closed.

The City Council heard the speakers, and decided not to close this Fire Station. The vote by the elected officials was unanimous to oppose the closing of this Fire Station, the oldest Fire Station in the City.

I went back to work with the department managers to think about other ways to balance the City's annual budget for the coming fiscal year!

LESSON SEVEN

OTHER CITY SERVICE

Departmental Services Change Over Time

A City's services change over time, and it is nice to document this trend in some of the municipal departments that every City in America has, like their Public Library.

For example, the city that I live in, and was their City Manager for several years, have documented how the public services in their library have changed over the years. Some of their major changes in the services that they provide to their city's citizens are highlighted below:

– The public library has increased its Spanish language book collection.
– Many public libraries now have their computer classes offered in Spanish
– Many public libraries have Bilingual Story times in Spanish for children that live in their city.
– The public libraries have removed books, due to the lack of their citizens use of them that were published in Polish, French, Italian, and German.
– The Children's room in many public libraries has been expanded to accommodate more seating and table arrangements.
– In the Library's Main Room, more desk-top computer have been added since more and more citizens are using them.
– The size of the Main Library has also been expanded over the years to accommodate additional space that were required to make the above changes.

Most City governments have several municipal departments, and they all change their respective public services over time, like the Library Department does.

While a City's Public Library reflects how City services change over time, they are only one example of how these public services change – which takes place in all City departments over the years!

While the citizens create these changes, their elected official approve them, and their city's staff implements them, and also recommends future changes to them as their city's population continues to change in the future!

Employee Job Interview Questions

Many years ago, when I was assigned to the Office of the City Manager, employee job interview questions were not restricted, and the employees on the Job interview Panel, could ask almost any questions that they wished of City job applicants.

In the early days, decades ago, when I started in the public sector, and was appointed to Job Interview Panel, one female applicant was asked the following questions by the male panelists. The applicant was a female that was applying for an analytical position in a city government.

Some members of this Job Interview Panel asked this female job applicant the following questions:

– I noticed that you had a "ring" on your left-hand. Does this mean that you are engaged to be married?

- Another Job Interview Panelist asked her when she was going to be married?
- Another Job Interview Panelist asked her, when she married, do you plan to have any children during the coming year?
- At this time, many years ago, they wanted to know this, since they wanted any employee that was hired to stay employed with the city forever once they were hired.

Such questions are now illegal, since special arrangements can be made for many circumstances, such as giving female employees time-off when their children are born, and to stay home with them and help raise them after they are born.

The types of questions that can be asked by an employer, like City officials, if someone is applying for a city position, are now quite limited, by local, state, and federal laws, which were approved to control the types of question that can be asked to prospective employees of any government – city, county, state, and federal.

Nowadays, no questions may be asked to any government job applicants, in the following area:

- It is improper to ask a prospective employee about their personal political affiliations.
- It is improper to ask a prospective employee about the religious affiliations, and
- It is improper to ask a prospective employee about their personal lives.

The types of questions asked b government officials to applicants of jobs in their respective organizations are now related to their personal qualifications, their job-related experience, and other job-related questions.

Limiting any personal questions about a job applicant's personal life, political affiliations, or religious affiliations are no longer appropriate.

This is a good thing, since you want to hire qualified employees, based on their professional qualifications!

Citizens Use of Public Property

Early in my public service career, when I worked in the Office of the City Manager, a complaint from one of our City Council members was given to me by the City Manager, and he asked me to follow up and respond to it.

An article was in our local newspaper noting that a group of citizens were going to gather in our major park, and advocate for same-sex couples, and that this was okay for a living arrangement, and that other citizens should agree with same-ex friendship trend.

The City Council member that contacted the City Manager wanted the city to stop this gathering in our city park, and wanted the city to prohibit it, since he did not want it to interfere with the movement of citizens in our city park, or pedestrians on our sidewalks next to the park, or the vehicles on the streets adjacent to this park.

This was a reasonable question from one of our elected officials, so I went to the City Attorney's Office to speak with one of our City Lawyers about this situation, and he related the following:

– Many citizens will be gathering in this city park, but they must not prevent other citizens from doing so,

– That can walk on the City's sidewalks, but they must not prevent regular citizens from walking on them, and

– They should not block any streets from citizens to drive their vehicles on.

When I met with a lawyer in our City Attorney's Office, he also related the following group meeting legal requirements to me:

– It is legal for citizens to meet in a public park, so long as they did not interfere with other citizens who wish to use our city park,

– It was legal for citizens to walk on City sidewalks, so long as they did not interfere with other citizens who wish to walk on them, and

– The members of such a group on City property could only cross streets legally, either at stop-lights, cross-walks, or other legal street crossings.

The major thing to watch-out for the City Lawyer said was that we do not want them to:

– Prevent citizens from being able to visit and use their city park, or

– Prevent citizens from being able to use the sidewalks around this city park, or

– Restrict the transportation of citizen vehicles on roadways next to this city park.

The City Lawyer said that, while it was legal for this group of citizens to meet on public property, that I should ask the Police Department to assign Police Officers to this area, when this group met, to make sure that other citizens have access to the city's park, its adjacent sidewalks, and the roadways that are next to our city park.

I told him that I would do this, and I informed the City Manager of this, and then asked the Chief of Police to assign some Police Officers as requested by this City Lawyer in the City Attorney's Office.

Everything worked well, and we had no problems!

Property Tax Collections

When I arrived as City Manager in a City, they had a relatively low Property Tax collection rate, I think that it was about 85 percent or so. I was meeting with the staff, and working on ways to increase this City's annual Property Tax Collection rate.

The Finance Director provided me with a list of those citizens that had not yet paid their annual Property Tax bill. There were dozens of names on this list, which showed the person's name, their address, and the amount of property taxes that they owed to the City. Their home address would be the piece of real property that they own that they have not yet paid their annual Property Taxes on.

The City's staff was going to make a list of the property owners, and place their respective names and addresses, and the amount of Property Taxes that they owed, in a paid column in our local newspaper. Everyone hoped that this would embarrass everyone on this list, and that they would all pay their Property Taxes promptly.

It was brought to my attention that one of the names on this list was our mayor, and that I should inform him of the fact that his name will appear on this list in our local newspaper if he did not pay his Property Taxes before this information was going to be published in our local newspaper.

I went down to the mayor's office, and talked to him, and related this information to him. He asked me to remove his name from this listing of property owners in our city that have not yet paid their respective Property Taxes.

My response to him was that, if I removed your name from this list, and a reporter at our local newspaper found out, that this information could wind-up as an article on the front page of our city's newspaper. I told him that I would never mention this, but that several other City employees know about this, and I would not want any one of them to tell a reporter of our city newspaper, and find this information as a front-page article.

He said that he would think about this, and that he would get back to me! Within a couple of days, the City's Property Tax Collector came to see me, and I was informed that the mayor had paid his real estate Property Taxes, so he would no longer be on this list. I went back to the mayor and thanked him for paying his Property Taxes, and I told him that his name had been removed from this list.

When this list appeared in our local newspaper, many of the citizens started to pay the Property Taxes on their real property, that consisted of the home that they and their family lived in. During the coming weeks, more and more citizens on his list paid their persona Property Taxes.

When I left the City years later, the City's Property Tax collection rate was well over 090 percent. It was good that the City's professional staff focused on property tax collection practices, like this one, and that these efforts all paid off over time.

It was the right thing to do, and all of the City's citizens benefited from this ongoing revenue-collection effort!

Regulating Business Locations

It was in the local newspaper one day that an X-rated business had applied to a property owner in the City to locate on a major commercial corner in our town. This story was on their front page!

A few days later, a lady came to my office to see me. She said that her family lived across the street from where this store wanted to locate, and that she did not want her children living across-the-street from an X-rated business like this.

She went on to say that such a business would have X-rated things in their windows to attract customers, and that she did not like the people who would go to such a store because her children were located just across the street from it.

I thanked her for letting me know these facts, and then I brought them to our City Attorney and asked him what he thought we should do to try to accommodate this lady's zoning request. She wanted the city to keep this business out of this vacant store, and that whatever we had to do would be appreciated.

The lawyer told me that, this is America and that we can't prohibit such businesses from locating in our city, but that we can regulate them with certain zoning and distance requirements, subject to City Council approval.

I asked him what distance requirements were, and he told me that it is legal to regulate the location of such business, and to keep them a certain number of feet from residential area, public schools, churches, City facilities, and similar distancing requirements from non-profit organizations, so long as such regulations are approved by the City Council before they locate to our community.

I worked with the City Attorney, and we came up with a proposed law that would preclude them from locating next to residentially zoned areas, a number of feet from public schools, a number of feet from churches, and a number of feet from other City facilities, including certain non-profit organizations.

The proposed legislation was presented to the City Council for their consideration, and they unanimously approved it at one of their public meetings

This business did not locate in our community but, rather sought a location in a neighboring community that did not have such regulations, so it was legal for this business to locate in the right zone, almost wherever they wanted to in other communities.

The lady that lived across the street from where this X-rated store was trying to locate, came back to my office to thank me. I thanked her for letting me know about this, and that what our city did was the right thing to do!

She, and other citizens, agreed that their city, and its elected officials, did the right thing!

Public Hearing Officer

In one City that I served as their City Manager, their City Charter noted that I was their City's Hearing Officer. I would be required to hold public meetings to listen to the complaints brought by department managers against selected employees that worked in their respective departments.

If a department manager wanted to discipline one of their employee for any wrongdoing, their request would be sent to the City's Hearing Officer, which was the City Manager. I would hold this public hearing since it was required.

This was unusual, since most City Managers re not lawyers, yet the City's Employee Unions would hire lawyers to represent their respective employees that were brought up on charges by our city's department managers.

Because of this, when I held these hearings as the Hearing Officer, I would ask the City Attorney to assign an Assistant City Attorney to be with e for each of these hearings.

I would listen to the lawyers that the Employee Unions hired to represent their employees brought up on charges, and after these hears, when the employee and their lawyer left the public hearing, I would have a number of days to respond to their respective presentations.

I would always ask the Assistant City Attorney that was present with me during these hearings, to let me know what I should do? This meant, prepare a draft letter for me to sign, review, and send it to our Employee Union's lawyer, who represented the employee that the public hearing was being held for.

From a legal standpoint, I always felt like I was doing the right thing! And every time that I responded to the Union's attorney, they would be satisfied with my response, and I would never hear back from them, until their next employee's hearing.

While I was the Hearing Officer, it helped me greatly having an Assistant City Attorney with me every time that I held these hearings.

I did the right thing, no employee union's lawyer ever questioned any of my decisions. So, I felt that I was doing the right thing with the City's Assistant City Attorney's assistance, which I use consistently for several years!

Employee Health Benefits Audit

There was a national trend several years ago, for Cities to have Health Insurance Audits done on their respective employees. This would make sure that they were not abusing their respective health care benefits, and this service was performed by an independent private Employee Health Insurance Auditing Company.

I asked my Mayor and City Council to approve a contract with one of these private companies, and they unanimously approved our city's contract with an independent private firm to perform this service for our city.

The Presidents of the Employee Unions, were all informed of this service, and each of them notified their respective employees. This study was done to make sure that no employees were abusing or taking advantage of their City Council-approved employee health benefits.

Some employees did not like this study being done, and when the study was done, I received a report from this company on our City's Health Benefits Audit. It took a couple of months to do this study and, when it was done, the city received the following information on our employees and the health benefits that they were receiving.

Some of the findings of this health benefits audit revealed the following information:

– Some employees had their previous spouse still covered by their health benefits,
– Some employees had their previous children covered by their health benefits,
– A few employees had some of their children covered, even though they were too old to receive this health benefit,
– Other employees had their college-age children receiving their health benefit, even though they were never enrolled in college, and
– Other employees had a spouse that was employed and receiving health benefits, but they charged their health services to the policy with the best benefits – even if it was their spouse's City health plan.

For some of these health benefit violations, employees had to pay back the city for any illegal charges that they had made to the City's health benefits plan.

Some employee's former spouses, children, and children not in college, or too old to go to college, were also charged to pay back the city for these illegal health benefits that they had been receiving.

When this study was done, the listing of each employee, and their eligible health benefit recipients – their spouse, children, and illegal charges to the City's health plan, had to be reimbursed to the City.

This was a good thing to do, and employees, and their dependents, were adjusted, including qualified college-age students, so that everyone eligible was receiving what they should be in their respective health benefit plan from the City.

This was a great study to undertake, and the citizens saved a lot of money after this process was done!

Trees on Our Main Street

In one city that I was their City Manager, they had a Main Street in their downtown that had no trees on it Other neighboring communities around us also had Main Streets, but they had trees on all of their respective Main Streets.

I meet with the City's staff, in the Public Works Department, and we decided that we would place the funds to purchase these trees and install them on our Main Street in our City's budget for the coming year.

The City Council held budget review sessions, and when they reviewed the Public Works Department budget, the staff (the City Manager and the Public Works Director) explained to them that we had funds in this budget to purchase and plant trees on our Main Street.

We felt that our citizens went to Main Streets in other cities because it was nicer to shop there, and that if we planted trees on the Main Street in our downtown, that maybe more citizens from neighboring communities would come to our city to shop there.

The City's elected officials (their Mayor and City Council) unanimously approved the city budget that had these expenses (to purchase and plant these trees on our Main Street) in it.

After this City budget was approved, a few months later, our Public Works Department purchased these trees, and its staff began to make arrangements to plant them on the Main Street in our downtown area.

A few days after this project was started, the mayor came to me and told me that our downtown merchants were coming to him and asking him why we were planting trees on our Main Street, since as they grew, they would block their respective business signs, and citizens would not be able to read them.

This was a good question, and I explained to the mayor that the City Council approved our annual budget with funds to purchase and install these trees on our Main Street in it.

I also told him that our public works staff would trim these trees, so that they would not block the signs of businesses on our Main Street.

I also told him that, in the future years, as these trees grew in size, that we would make sure that they would never block the viewing of our Main Street business signs so citizens could not read them.

In closing, I mentioned to the mayor, that if any business person has any questions, that he/she should ask them to call me, and I would explain our Main Street tree planting process to them.

Our goal was to improve nature in our downtown, so that maybe citizens from other neighboring communities would come to our city to do their downtown shopping.

Accommodating the Homeless

One yar I went to an Annual City Managers Conference in Portland, Oregon, one of the greatest cities in the northwest portion of our nation. It is one of the most populated cities in the northwest section of our nation, while Seattle, Washington, is the most populated city.

My conference was held in their downtown area, and I stayed in a hotel that was not too far from the Willamette River. It was wonderful staying at a local hotel that was so close to this river, which I could walk to in the morning and the evening during my stay in their great City.

The City of Portland is not on the Oregon Coast, since it is located sixty miles inland from the Pacific Ocean. While you never see the ocean when you are staying in Portland, you certainly can see some wonderful local rivers.

Portland has two major rivers, with many bridges that go across them so that their citizens can take their cars to different portions of their community. As a matter of fact, some folks call the City of Portland, "Bridgetown," because of the many bridges that they have in their city.

I would walk by the river by my hotel, before and after my conference, so I could see it in the morning and later in the evening. Their river was beautiful all of the time, both in the morning and in the evening. I enjoyed my walk by it all of the time!

One morning, before my conference, I walked by their downtown river, early in the morning since I enjoyed it so much. When it turned eight o'clock in the morning, I heard the following.

A Police Officer walked to the middle of the park, where there was a large flag pole, and he hit his baton on it several times, trying to wake people up that were sleeping in the park.

H then said, it is now eight o'clock in the morning, and the city would like all of you to wake up, and remove your sleeping things, since the tourists in our city will be coming here soon, and we do not want them to see the homeless people in our park.

The people sleeping in the park got up, picked-up their sleeping materials – blankets, sleeping bags, pillows, and related materials, and removed them so that the incoming tourists would not see that this park was occupied by homeless people during the previous evening.

I thought that this was Great! Homeless people could stay in this park, and that was alright with the city, but that they should wake-up and get out of the park in the morning so that the many folks, like me, can come to visit their community, and view their wonderful river park without having to see any of their homeless people in it.

I thought that this was a great City – Portland, Oregon! They could accommodate the homeless, with some restrictions, and make their parks available to their many City visitors, from throughout our nation, like me.

I also thought that this was a wonderful policy, since the City could accommodate their tourist, but also provide overnight sleeping facilities for their homeless population!

Processing Citizen Complaints

When I was serving as a City Manager in one City, a citizen came to see me one day, and he said that he hired a private contractor to do some work for him, and that he used immigrant employees that he had picked-up on the corner of one of our city's streets in the immigrant citizen portion of our city.

He related the following information to me, which this person thought was illegal, and he wanted me to follow-up on his request to solve these legal violation problems.

This citizen related the following information to me:

- This contractor picked up some immigrant citizens on the corner of one of the streets in our downtown area,
- They were not legal citizens, and he hired them to do contracting work for his company,
- He also said that he did not pay them the legal minimum wage,
- He paid them in cash, and did not deduct any State taxes from his payments to them, and
- That he also did not deduct any Federal taxes from his payments to them.

He said that this was against the law, and he wanted me to direct our Police Officers to keep these immigrant citizens off of our downtown streets, since these citizens are being picked up to do work, and the contracting company's owner was not following our State and Federal laws when he did this.

I checked with our City Attorney, who said that it was not against the law for any of our citizens, including immigrant ones, to stand on the city's street corners in our downtown area. He also related that:

- The legal requirement to pay an employee the minimum wage was a state law,
- The legal requirement to pay State Taxes on an employee's wages was also a state law, and
- The legal requirement to pay Federal Taxes on an employee's wages was a federal law.

The City Attorney said that the legal violations brought up by this citizen were not City violations, but rathe State and Federal government legal violations.

He told me to give the citizen, that complained about these items, the contact information for his State and Federal government elected representatives. He could contact them, and ask them to follow-up on these legal violations, since these were not City legal violations, but rather State and Federal government legal violations.

I met with the citizen that complained about these problems, and I encouraged him to contact his elected State and Federal government representatives, and I gave him their names, official titles, and their telephone numbers. He thanked me and said that he would follow-up accordingly!

The Imprisonment Process

One time, during my public service career as a City Manager, a citizen was released from prison and came to see me at my office in City Hall. My secretary said to me that. He wanted to talk to me about how he was arrested.

He came to my office, and told me about the fact that he was a drug dealer, and that when he was arrested and brought to our Police Department, that he had over one-thousand dollars in his wallet, which was taken from him, before he was placed in jail.

So, when he got out of jail, he received things back that were taken from him when he was arrested, but that the money that he had in his wallet, over one-thousand dollars, was not given back to him, and he wanted to know why – and where it went!

He explained his arrest story to me, and what he received back when he was released from prison. He said that he wanted his one-thousand dollars back, since it was his, and that it was in his wallet at the time he was arrested.

I went to the City Attorney, located down the hall from my office, explained this to him and he told me to have this person write down what happened to him when he was arrested, and what was taken from him, and what was not given back to him when he was released from prison. He said that he should date and sign this document.

He did that, and I gave his statement to the City Attorney, and we both talked about this in a Closed Session at a future City Council meeting. We both asked the City Council for money to have an Internal Audit done on our arresting process, and what would have happened to the money that was taken from and never returned to this person.

The City Council approved funds to have this Internal Audit done, and when it was done it was determined that the Police Officer that received the person property from people that were arrested, had received these funds, but that they were never given back to them when they were released from prison.

The Internal Audit was done, and it was documented that the funds that were taken from this person when he was arrested but they were never given back to him, and that the only person that could have taken them was the Police Officer that was in charge of this police process.

I went back to the City Council and told them that I was terminating this Police Officer for personally taking these funds, and other things, from citizens that were arrested, and turned over all of their personal property at the time of their arrest to this Police Officer.

Another Police Officer was appointed by the Chief of Police to serve in this capacity, and this problem never happened again, at least during my tenure as their City Manager.

It was great to have an Internal Audit done by an independent out side agency in order to document this process, and to find out the facts about what happened to these funds. This is the role of government, to do the right thing!

More Minority Police Officers

Early in my public service career, I worked in a large city with a very diverse population. I worked in the Office of the City Manager, and the Police Department was one of the departments that was assigned to me to work with.

I kept hearing comments that we had almost no minority Police Officers. Everywhere that I went citizens made these comments, so it concerned me, so one day I contacted the Chief of Police and related the following information.

I told the Chief of Police that many citizens ask me why our city does not have more minority Police Officers, since the population of our city has such a large minority population. The Chief of Police thought about this for a while, and responded to me as follows.

I have only been the Chief of Police for a few years, and I would agree with you. One thing that you have to keep in mind is that you have to wait for the old non-minority Police Officers to retire before you can hire more Police Officers, which I would like to be minority Police Officers too.

So, the Chief of Police and I agreed on this topic! I related this to the City Manager, and he also agreed with this statement. So, over the years, as non-minority Police Officers retired, or moved on, the city would hire more and more minority Police Officers.

When I would talk to various organizations in the city, since the City Manager would ask me to, I would relate this information to them. Also, many of these organizations had many minority members that belonged to them.

Again, I would always say that a community changes quicker than its city government does, and that we have to wait for the older non-minority employees to retire before we can hire more minority city employees and this goes for all of our city departments.

Everyone that I talked to always agreed that we were doing the right thing, and that, in all of the city's departments, we had to wait for the old non-minority employees to retire before we could hire more minority employees.

Our goal was, I would tell our citizens, was to have the nature of the city's workforce be the same as the ethnic composition of our community – but that I would take a while to do this. All of the citizens were always pleased that we agreed with this ongoing hiring practice!

Over the years the city had more-and-more minority employees, and everyone was proud of this – the Mayor and City Council, the City Manager, and all of the City's Department Managers.

We all felt that we were doing the right thing!

LESSON EIGHT

OTHER CITY TOPICS

Citizen Request to Hold Down Property Taxes

The city's annual budget, in one city that I worked in, was presented annually to the public in a local high school auditorium. The Mayor and City Council set up these meetings to inform the citizens of their city's proposed budget for the coming fiscal year.

When I was done making the city's budget presentation, there was a Question & Answer period, to allow citizens a chance to ask questions about the proposed budget. One of the best, general, questions asked was from a female senior citizen, who asked the following question

I've lived in this city for many years, and the property taxes on my house have gone up every year. They have never gone down. Are you going to do anything as our new City Manager to try to hold our property taxes down in future years?

I responded that I just moved to their city, and that my family just purchased a house. I told the citizens that I'm telling them this because I, like them, don't like paying property taxes either, and that I would not want them going up each year forever, year-after-year.

I said watch my city budgets in future years, and that I promise you that I will do everything I can to keep your property taxes down. The audience applauded!

After one or two more of these Annual Public Meetings, they were never held again during my tenure as their City's City Manager. This is because I always, every fiscal year, tried to prepare the lowest budget possible to hold down property taxes for everyone in this city!

Citizen Taxation Request

The city that I was a City Manager in, had a chapter of a national senior citizens association, and they would hold monthly meetings in the conference room of a local non-profit organization. At one of their meetings, I was asked to be their Guest Speaker. They wanted me to fill about an hour of time, which I did.

I talked about the city, its budget and operations, and at the end of my presentation some of their members asked me some questions.

When I was done with the City Manager's presentation at their meeting, there were a few great questions, that I will highlight below, including my response to it.

One male senior citizen, a resident of the city, said that he pays his annual Property Taxes, which include financing the costs of our city's children going to their local public schools – elementary, middle schools (called junior high schools in the olden days), and high schools.

The bottom-line of his question was that, I don't have any children at home, since they are all grown up now, so why do I continue to have to pay property taxes for the cost of young people going to our public schools, when I do not use this public service. I paid for years, but I should not pay any more, since I do not use this service, since my children are all grown-up now.

After some quick introspective reflection, I responded to this person as follows. Sir, it costs about $13,000 a year per student for them to go to their respective public schools. This was an average per student cost for their city's public education. I reiterated that it costs $13,000 per student each year for them to go to a city school, and all property owners in our city pay these expenses in their respective annual property taxes.

I told him that I pay this mount too, in the property taxes that I personally pay to the city every year. I told him that I do not have any children in our schools either, but that I do not mind paying this annual cost, especially because of the following information that I just read about in our state's newspaper.

I said that our state's newspaper just ran a story that it costs the citizens in our State $40,000 a year to pay for a citizen to be in a State Prison, and we have no control over the fact that they spend our State Income Taxes that we pay to our State for these annual jail-maintenance expenses.

I went on to say that, I'd rather pay $13,000 a year for a student to go to school, since they are likely to go on to college, get a better job, make a higher income, buy a better house, and then they pay their respective property taxes to the city for years to come.

This way, we all get our money back, by holding down our property taxes in future years.

On the other hand, many of the citizens in prison are high school dropouts, never went to college, never held a good job, may have never purchased a house, and have never paid any property taxes. This is why the citizens of our state, including me and you, pay $40,000 annually per inmate to keep a citizen in one of our State Prisons.

I told him that I'd rather pay $13,000 per year to educate our young people, rather than $40,000 a yar to keep a high-school dropout in prison – for sometimes many years.

He thanked me for my comments, and told me that he agreed with me!

Senior Citizens and Property Taxes

There are various residential development practices evolving that will hold down the amount of property taxes that other citizens have to pay on their personal residences. These senior citizen residential development practices seem politically logical, and must be approved by a city's elected officials to become residential development laws in a city.

For example, a City Council where I was the new City Manager, had previously approved special density residential developments for senior citizens that could be built in their city, depending upon the zoning laws that were also approved of the City's Planning Commission.

Such new residential developments, where only citizens over a certain age usually older adults, could live were sought for the following reasons:

— The citizens that purchase these residential units usually do not have children, so when a person or couple buys a house/condominium in such a residential development, the city knows that it does not have to worry about an increase in their educational expenses.
— The city also knows that, since such couples don't have any children, that they would not have any additional young people using their municipal swimming pool local neighborhood parks, and young people sports facilities.
— These citizens have sufficient funds to pay for these units, because of their age, and the City knows that it would not have to hire any new Police Officers, since such citizens as this seldom commit any crimes or violations of any local laws.

For these reasons, City Councils in cities throughout our nation adopt building requirements for such senior citizens residential developments. Such legal actions by elected officials would establish an age limit for those citizens that purchase residential units in residential projects of this nature.

If desired by a City Council, a City's Planning Commission can make recommendations to their elected officials to adopt such residential development restrictions in various residential zones within a city. These revised laws, however, must also be approved by the City Council.

The bottom-line is that the property taxes are as high as the other residential homes in the area, but the level of public services provided by the city for these new residents is a lot less then those citizen that live in other homes that were built in the past under their city's regular residential zoning requirement.

Avoiding Vehicle Taxes

In one city where I was a City Manager, someone once introduced me to a person that had out-of-state license plates on all his family's personal vehicles, as well as the various vehicles that were used for his business.

This person did not have to register his business in our State, and once his business was registered in another State, he did not have to pay annual Vehicle Taxes on his personal cars, and the various vehicles used by the employees that worked for his company.

I asked a City Attorney how this could take place, and he responded that the owner of this company registered his company in another State, one with no Vehicle Taxes, like our State has. He also had a mailing address in the other State and he could register all of his vehicles to this out-ot-state address.

This person did not have to pay State taxes on his personal business, since it was registered in another State, and this State did not have Vehicle Taxes, like our State did, so the owner of this company did not have to pay these taxes either.

It was all legal, and this person saved a lot of money every year that he would have to spend if he had to pay State Income tax on his business, and pay a City Vehicle Tax on all of his cars and trucks that were registered to his company, out of State.

Seems like States should have State laws to prevent these type of tax avoidance opportunities. Citizens that live in a state and a city in the State should have to register their company and its vehicles in the State and City that the person lived in.

This would be the right thing for every State in our Nation to do!

Personal Property Taxes

When I was a City Manager, I knew a very successful business person, who lived in a neighboring community, and I noticed that on his two vehicles that he had out-ot-state license plates on both of them.

While many States don't have a Personal Vehicle Tax, some of them do. Such a Personal Property Tax is approved by each State's elected officials. Some states allow a city to have both Real Property Taxes and Personal Property Taxes on citizen-owned vehicle(s).

He was a very successful business person, and I asked him how does he get to have out-of-state license plates on his family's personal vehicles. He told me that he and his wife own second-homes in two other States, one down south, and one up north.

He went on to state that neither one of these States have a Personal Property Tax on personal vehicles, in his family's case automobiles. He said that he and his wife did not have to pay this tax since they had license plates on both of them, and that they were from other States that did not have such a tax.

He said that, legally he was supposed to live in another State for six-months a year to qualify for this State to be his family's legal residence. He said that they do not, and that no States check-out this residency information to make sure that this requirement is complied with.

While I pay my State's Persona Property Tax on my personal car, and almost everyone that I know does the same, some people who own second-homes in other States know how to avoid their respective Stat's tax on their personal vehicles.

They know how to save money, and they know that they will never get caught! Seems like States should check such vehicle registrations to make sure that the recipient actually, and legally, does live in their respective State for a minimum of six-months a year.

While I always pay my property taxes, some people know how to avoid some of them, and they also know that they will never get caught for not paying them.

This is not right, and States should enforce their legal residency requirements. This would help all States that have a Personal Vehicle Tax!

Privatization of Public Services

In many cities that I have worked in, there was a desire to contract-out selected public services to the private sector. Sometimes this subject was brought-up by the mayor, members of the City Council, the City Manager, and sometimes the Department Managers.

There are many regulations that govern a city's ability to contract-out selected public services. For example:

– The Mayor and City Council wanted me to contract-out janitorial and landscaping services, which were services provided by our city employee. I learned that there was a clause in the City-Union Labor Agreement noting that it is against the rules to contract-out any public services that are performed by any of the union's employees. This Labor Agreement had been approved by the former Mayor and City Council, and was a legal document until it is changed in the future.

– A citizen that owned a private security company said that the City could contract with his company to patrol the City's parks and sports facilities. He would charge the city about one-third of what a Police Officer would make performing this same work. The City Attorney remined me of a State Law, which was lobbied for by the State Police Unions decades ago, and that any police related work in our State can only be done by a sworn Police Officer. This was a State Law!

There were other public services where it was common to contract out for them. Many cities contracted out the following services to the private sector.

- If a Traffic Engineering Study is needed the City contracts with a private engineering company for such services. The in-house City Engineer is not qualified to do this type of engineering work.
- If any Geotechnical Engineering work is needed, the typical City would contract out this technical engineering service to a private engineering company. Again, the in-house City Engineer would not be qualified to do this type of technical engineering work.
- Almost every City contracts-out their annual auditing services to a private sector auditor to do their Annual City Audit. It is typically in a City Charter to require that this type of service must be performed by an outside private auditing company.
- Also, it is common, if a city wants to have Management Study done, it would contract out this type of service to a Private Consulting Company. You don't want such a study done by any City employees.

So, the types of public services that a City can contract-out for would depend upon existing State Laws, and City-Union Labor Agreements that prohibit a City from contracting-out any public services provided by their Union members, the City employees that belong to this Union.

Doing What Is Right — Getting A City Building Permit

Once when I was a City Manager, I was about to have some work done on my house, since the roof on my house was very old and had to be replaced. I received a proposal from a contractor to perform this work, and I told him to go ahead and do it.

He was going to start on a Saturday, since I wanted to be home when he started this work. So, on the Saturday that he arrived, he was ready to perform this work. Prior to him starting, I asked him if he had received a City Building Permit.

The contractor told me that he did not, but that I should not worry about it. He said that the City that I lived in did not have enough Building Inspectors, so he would not get caught, since the City would not catch him breaking the legal requirement for not getting a Building Permit.

I told him that I was the City Manager, and that I am requiring him to get a City Building Permit, since he must follow the law when performing work on my house. I said that if he did not get a City Building Permit, and someone found out, and informed the local newspaper, that I would end up on their front page with an article about me allowing a contractor to do work on my house without receiving a legally required City Building Permit.

H said that if he did get a Building Permit, that he would just raise the amount that he was charging me, since the cost of the Building Permit was not included in the cost estimate that he gave me, and that I previously approved for him to do the work on my house.

I told him to get the City Building Permit, place the of it on the bill he will give me for performing the work on my house, and that I would be happy to pay for it.

He got the City Building Permit, did the work, I paid his fee, and everyone did the right thing!

Speaking to Prisoners at the Prison

While serving as a City Manager, I was asked to speak to prisoners at a Regional State Prison. The community that I was City Manager of was located in the same County that the prison was located.

I spoke to about 50 prisoners for about an hour. My topic focused on going to night school while working full-time to get a good education and job to become successful in life.

My focus was on my background! I grew up as a kid in a blue-collar family, and after my high school graduation, like all of my friends, I joined the military service. I served for four years in the U.S. Coast Guard.

I told them that, when I was in the military, I had an office job, went to night school, and before I "got out" of the service I had earned an Associate Degree from a local two-year college. Then I told them that I went to night school on the G.I. Bill for over fourteen years, obtaining a Bachelor of Science Degree, M.P.A. Degree, M.B.A. Degree, and a Ph.D. Degree. The same month that I received my doctoral degree I was appointed as a City Manager.

I stressed the need for hard-work and focusing on your educational goals to become successful.

After my speech, several prisoners came up to where I was to ask me some questions. When each one was done, I asked them "why are you here, what did you do to have to go to prison."

Each one responded to my question as follows:

The First Prisoner – I'm here for stabbing someone in a fight, but it was not true. While I was holding a knife, the person I was fighting jumped on it during our fight, so he really stabbed himself. So, I should not be here.

The Second Prisoner – I am here for shooting someone during a fight that we were having. In reality, I was holding a gun, but he tried to grab it, and by accident he pressed my trigger finger and the gun went off, so he actually shot himself. So, I should not be here either.

The Third Prisoner – I was in a park on the grass and, during our fight, I hit him in the head and he moved off the grass on to the concrete sidewalk, and then fell down. This fall did serious damage to him, and that is why I am in jail. I thought he would fall on the grass, but instead, he walked onto the sidewalk and fell on the concrete. So, I should not be here either.

Because of these response, I felt like each prisoner had a reason that they were in the prison but that they really should not be there because of their individual interpretations of their respective violations of the law.

I then "wished all of them my best," and left the room, got in my car, and drove back to work.

This was my one-hour experience from speaking to prisoners at the Regional State prison

A Wonderful Meeting at a Conference

Many years ago, when I was at an Annual City Managers Conference in the City of San Antonio, Texas, I went one day early to attend a training session. There were about a hundred local government folks at this meeting. All sitting at round tables with several people around each one.

When the training session stopped for lunch, we all ate at the same location that we sat at during the training session. During this lunch time, I got to meet the gentleman that was sitting next to me.

We both introduced ourselves to each other, and he went on to explain that he was an immigrant to the State of Texas from Mexico. He went on to explain his background to me. He went on to state that:

– His mom and dad snuck across the border when he was a young boy,
– They lived on a man's farm, and his mom and dad did farm-work over the years,
– He said that he went to local public schools as a child, and
– When he graduated from high school,
– Then when he graduated from high school, he attended a local public university,
– He just said that a few weeks ago that he took the State's Bar Examination to become a lawyer,
– And that he just received a notice that he had passed it, and
– Now he is a lawyer in the State of Texas!

He went on to tell me that he could not have done what he did in Mexico, and that he was so glad that his mom and dad brought their family to the State of Texas when he was a young boy.

He went on to tell me, and ended his statement, with the comment that, he was proud to be an American and that he thought that the United States was "The Land of Opportunity," and that he was a living example of it.

I told him that it was a pleasure to meet him, and that I knew that he was going to have a very successful legal career in the City of San Antonio, in the State of Texas.

This is one immigrant that was certainly proud to be an American, and I was very pleased to have met him and to have heard about his background!

This was a learning experience for me about immigrants, their achievements from doing hard work, and how much they liked America!

The Name of a Major University

Once, several years ago, I was attending an annual City Manager Conference in the City of Chicago, and in the morning, I was walking around in their downtown area, prior to attending my conference sessions.

I notice a major university in their downtown area, and I looked to read its title and it said Northwestern University. I said to myself, wow, I am not in the State of Washington or the State of Oregon, so why would this school be called Northwestern University.

This bothered me, so I did some research, and found the following facts:

— The Northwest Territory was approved in 1787, when this was the northwestern portion of the United States. It was part of our nation's western expansion during this time in our history.
— The school was an old one, and it was formed in 1851, when it was actually located in the Northwest Territory of the United States. Hence the reason for its name.
— Years later this area became known as the Old Northwest portion of our nation.

I always learned a lot when I attended my Annual City Manager Conferences over the years, but this was one of the most important things that I learned during this annual conference session.

Now I know why this school is called Northwestern University, since it was actually named when it was in the Northwestern portion of our nation.

I assume that the citizens of the City of Chicago know this, but people from outside of their state, like me, usually would not know this.

Later in my life I felt that now I can move to the City of Chicago, since I know so much about it!

Where the Alamo is Located

I attended an Annual City Manager conference several years ago in the City of San Antonio. Once I checked into my hotel, and walked to my room, I looked out the window in my room down onto the surrounding area.

I saw a bunch of old buildings, especially on building not far from my hotel that had a roof on it that looked like it was decades old. When I saw this, I wondered where I was, and I thought that maybe I was in the old part of their city.

Later, I was downstairs, and walked up to the Hotel's Main Desk and asked the Desk Clerk, there are a bunch of old buildings next to this hotel, and especially one with a very aging roof that looked like it was many years old, and it is not far from this hotel!

She told me, the building that you are looking at outside of the window in your hotel room is The Alamo, and our hotel is located in The Alamo Plaza Historic District in the City of San Antonio.

She went on to say the following about what is now commonly called the Alamo:

— It was formerly called The Mission San Antonio de Valero,
— She said it was the site of the Battle of the Alamo between Texas and Mexico in 1836,
— Now The Alamo is a public Museum in the Alamo Plaza Historic District, That, over four million visitors a year come to visit this site, and that
— It is one of the most popular historic sites in America.

Once I heard this information, I knew that my hotel was not located on the old part of town, but that it was located in The Alamo Plaza Historic District, and I was proud to be staying at a hotel in this area, since my Annual City Manager Conference was only a few blocks away.

Based on this information about The Alamo, I enjoyed my time at this Annual City Manager Conference, and spent many off-duty conference hours walking around the City of San Antonio's downtown historical area.

Later in life, when I visited the State of Texas, I would always drive to the City of San Antonio, to walk by the San Antonio River, and to see their downtown Alamo Plaza Historic District.

The Size of Central Park

Several years ago, I went to New York City to attend an Annual City Manager Conference in Manhattan. Once I went to this conference, and had some time off in the evenings, and once in a while in the afternoons, I would explore the Borough of Manhattan – since it is located on a New York City Island.

One day, with a few available hours in the afternoon, I walked up to Central Park, and started to walk around it. It was wonderful and I enjoyed it greatly!

I was going up the west side of Central Park, and was walking for a long time, and finally I wondered – how large is this park?

I had a map of Manhattan, and I looked at it, and realized the following:

- The Park has a northern boundary on 110th Street, and a southern boundary on 59th Street,
- The Park has a western boundary on 8th Avenue, and an eastern boundary on 5th Avenue,
- This means that Central Park in the Borough of Manhattan, New York City, is 2.5 miles long and .5 miles wide, and
- This would require that if I walked around this park, that it would be a six miles walk, and take me many hours to do.

When I found this out, I realized that I had been walking for well over two hours, and that there was no way that I could walk around this City of New York Park, located in the Borough of Manhattan, called Central Park.

After all, it is one of the largest inner-city parks in America, and I did not know this before I started my weekday walk around it.

Also, I later found out that this inner-city park has over 38 million visitors annually, and that it is managed by the Central Park Conservancy, which was created in 1980 to manage this beautiful New York City Park.

Over the years, almost every time that I have visited New York City, which was especially frequent when I lived in New Jersey for several years, I would explore and visit different portions of this wonderful park in the Borough of Manhattan, but never did I completely walk around it!

Most people do not know that the City of New York has five boroughs – they are the Boroughs of Bronx, Brooklyn, Manhattan, Queens and Staten Island.

New York City is in a great geographic location, and I would encourage other people to visit the City of New York, as well as all of its boroughs! I would encourage you to walk around them and to enjoy them all!

LESSON NINE

THE FUTURE

City Politics Change Over Time

In one City that I served as their City Manager for several years, I realized how City politics change over time. This City had several major political changes over the years.

When I arrived the Mayor and City Council consisted of primarily males that were middle-aged and senior citizens, who would run for the elected positions of Mayor and City Council. There were no females or minorities on the City Council when I arrived.

There were no Third-Party candidates, few Republican candidates, since they were almost always Democrats, and this is what the City was known for – since it consisted mostly of citizens that were registered to vote with the Democratic Party.

About a decade later the City had some female City Council members, some minority City Council members, a Republican would get elected to office now and then, and they even had a We the People Political Party member.

So, the political environment changes over time, and City Managers must operate in a political environment that changes from a gender, racial, age, and political perspective.

I would always tell new Mayors and City Council members that I was an Unaffiliated Voter, and that whoever was elected to office was my boss, and that I respected all of them since they were elected by our citizens to serve them.

They were all my boss, whoever was elected to the positions of Mayor and City Council, and they appointed me, and I always would do what they wished me to do by their majority vote.

This is how democracy works in a municipal government, and lowest form of government in our Nation!

Most citizens relate to this form of government, since many of them have gone to their respective City Council meetings, but I never knew anyone that would drive to their State Capitol to attend any public meetings, or go to our Nation's Capital to attend any federal government public meetings.

Most citizens directly relate to their municipal government much more than they do to their higher levels of government – their respective State government or our national government!

Homeland Security and Our Nation's Cities

After the terrorist attack that took place in our nation on September 11, 2001 (9/11/01), President Bush formed the Office of Homeland Security, which was led by the Assistant to the President.

One year later, in 2002, the U.S. Congress approved the Homeland Security Act, which formed the Department of Homeland Security (DHS). This was the newest federal department in many years, and was created and designed to improve the safety of cities and states throughout our nation, so another event like the one that took place on 9/11/01 would never happen again!

Since this was a new field, homeland security, I started collecting articles on evolving best practices in this new, dynamic, and rapidly evolving field. The early books that I wrote/edited in this field included the following:

Roger L. Kemp

- *Homeland Security: Best Practices for Local Government,*
- *Homeland Security for Citizens and Public Officials,*
- *Emergency Management and Homeland Security, and*
- *Homeland Security for the Private Sector.*

When the Department of Homeland Security was formed, the White House staff called a one-time meeting of national experts in this new filed to a meeting so that they could learn about best practices, and I was honored to be one of the homeland security experts invited to attend this important meeting.

There were about a dozen experts in this new field invited to attend this meeting, and we were asked to provide the White House Staff with information about the latest best practices in this field, so they would know how to organize the newly formed Department of Homeland Security.

I thought about what I would say at this meeting for many hours, and finally narrowed down my presentation to the following three homeland security best practice areas that I felt that our federal government should implement in their newly formed Department of Homeland Security. My suggestion were as follows:

- Several large cities on both coasts of the United States have international ports, with foreign ships going in-and-out of them every day throughout the year. We needed to know what ships were coming in, what they were carrying and/or picking-up, to make these ports safe for the citizens who lived in these international port cities.
- Many large cities in our nation have an international airport, where airplanes from other countries throughout the world fly and land at, and drop off and pick up people, then fly all over the world. All of these planes have a home nation that they are from. We need to enhance security at these international airports to make them safe for all of the citizens that use them.
- Lastly, those cities with large federal buildings and federal government monuments located in them should be monitored to ensure their safety. Nowadays, there is no underground parking at these federal facilities, and even on-the-street parking areas around these federal buildings and monuments do not have any more public parking areas. These steps have made our federal buildings and federal monuments a safer place to work at for their employees, and for the citizens that go to these facilities, including those citizens that visit our federal monuments.

It has been nearly 20 years since 9/11/01, and our nation has never had another terrorist attack as we did nearly a fifth of a century ago in downtown New York City. Our newest Federal Government department, the Department of Homeland Security, is doing a great job, and we all should encourage them to keep-up-the-good-work in future years!

I was honored to have been asked to share-my-thoughts when this new federal department was formed, and I thought that our federal government did the right thing by calling together some national experts in this new field so that they could share their thoughts on possible best practices that they should implement in the future, which they did!

America is now a safer place, even for those citizens that work at and visit our federal buildings, as well as those citizens that visit our nation's federal monuments!

Homeland Security and Our State's Cities

In the State of Connecticut, not to long after the terrorist incident on September 11, 2001 (9/11/01) our Governor formed a State Homeland Security Advisory Committee. I was asked to be on it because I had written/edited some books in this new, dynamic, and evolving field.

He appointed the following types of members to this Committee:

- A representative from the Federal Bureau of Investigation (FBI)
- A representative from the Federal Central Intelligence Agency (CIA)
- A representative from the Federal Military Service,
- A representative Chief of Police from a local Police Department,
- A representative Fire Chief from a local Fire Department, and
- A representative City Manager from one of the larger cities in our State.

I was the City Manager representative appointed by the Governor, due to the fact that I sent the Governor one of my first books titled *Homeland Security: Best Practices for Local Government*, which was a good thing, both for me as well as the State Homeland Security Advisory Committee.

I attended their meetings, which were held about once a month and, when we got together, we talked about how to make our State and its cities safer from a homeland security perspective.

Two important topics come to mind from our meetings! One was that our State had one Nuclear Power Plant, and the State contracted-out some of the services used to maintain this facility (e.g., landscaping, janitorial services, ground maintenance, etc.). They said that if any service was contracted out, that the FBI had to do background checks on all of the private company's employees that provided such services.

This was because if a foreign terrorist wanted to blow-up our State's Nuclear Power Plant, that he would just have to get a job with the private company that provided services to this facility, and he would have immediate access to this plant. This was made a requirement so such an act of terrorism would never happen in our State.

I went to visit one City that had a Metro-North Transportation Station in it, and I found out the following:

- I parked in an illegal parking space, and no one said a thing to me,
- I walked through an open gate to where the trains were on the tracks,
- I even walked in some trains that were being worked on, and
- Some of their employees saw me, but no one ever said a thing to me.

Since such a major train station was vulnerable from a homeland security standpoint, I mentioned these facts at our next meeting, and within a few days the city where the train station was located assigned their Police Officers to walk-around this train station every day and night, 24/7, which made this train station a much safer place, and less vulnerable from a terrorist incident standpoint.

Centralized City Purchasing

In every City that I served in as a City Manager, the purchasing functions was always centralized. Each of these cities had a Purchasing Officer, and the Purchasing Function was this person's responsibility.

The Purchasing Function was typically located in the City's Finance Department, and consisted of a Purchasing Officer and one or two employees to perform this function.

This was normal, and the Purchasing Officer did the purchasing for all of the City's departments and, in the process, saved the city a lot of money through this centralized purchasing process.

In one City, as a City Manager, when I arrived, I found out that each department manager was doing their own purchasing for their own respective departments.

Each department manager was purchasing their own business cards, departmental stationery, computers, and related goods and services, used in their respective departments throughout the year.

I reviewed this process, and it was different than any other City that I had worked in during my public service career as a City Manager over the years, typically in other States throughout our nation.

I mentioned this to the Mayor and City Council, and I told them that I should centralize this function as this is how this service was performed in most cities throughout our country. In most cities in America, the purchasing function is always centralized, usually within the Finance Department.

The Mayor and the City Council agreed with me, and this function was located as one of the functions within our City's Finance Department. While our city's department managers did not like this, since they were used to buying their own department products and services served the city well, since we purchased the same things, but at much lower price.

The City's Purchasing Officer was appointed by me, and this was included as one of the programs in our Finance Department, and they were happy to receive this program, since it would centralize this function, lower our costs for products and services, and help us save our taxpayers money during the year.

After a year, I reviewed this service, and the savings from centralizing our Purchasing Function, saved the city twice-as-much as it costs to hire a new Purchasing Officer, which was greatly appreciated by our taxpayers.

While the Mayor and City Council enjoyed this consolidation, saving the city a lot of money annually, many of the City's department manager's did not like it since they could no longer3 purchase their department's products and services that they wanted, personally.

A yar later, everyone was satisfied with this centralized Purchasing Function, including the Mayor and City Council, the City Manager, The City's department managers, as well as the citizens in our community – since it saved all of them annually, in the tax dollars that they paid to the city!

Making Your Shopping Mall Safer

When I was a City Manager of a City with a large City Shopping Mall not far from its downtown area, and close to a State Highway with on-ramps and off-ramps close to it, our city had a major automobile theft problem.

The Chief of Police reported it to me, the Shopping Mall Manager called me up about it, and the local newspaper did a front-page article about this problem. Personal automobiles were being stolen from the City Shopping Mall Public Parking lot, and the number of cars being stolen had been increasing.

The Chief of Police and I talked about this problem, and we agreed on the following facts that may be facilitating this stolen car trend:

- Local Police Departments attempt to solve crime problems in their respective cities,
- Our Shopping Mall was located just a minute or two from a major State Freeway, that
- Someone that stole a car from our City Shopping Mall could be on this State Highway in a short period of time, and
- Once the person with a stolen car was on the State Highway, they could be in several neighboring communities in just a few minutes.

This information was important, and this is why cars were being stolen from our City Shopping Mall, and not in other City shopping malls in neighboring communities.

This was because of the following reasons, which car theft criminals know all about:

- City Police Departments respond to crimes within their respective City limits,
- If someone drives a stolen car. On a State Highway, someone would have to call the State Police for them to pursue and resolve this crime,
- Once someone with a stolen car pulled off the State Highway, a Police Officer would have to call the City Police Department in the City that the stolen car was now located in, and
- Most importantly, who would do this?

After all, the owner of the stolen car could not do this, the Manager of our shopping mall could not do this, our Police Department could not do this – and this is why more-and-more personal vehicles were being stolen from our City Shopping Mall.

After talking with our Chief of Police about this problem, we jointly agreed on the following solution to this community problem, since fewer and fewer citizens were coming to our City's Shopping Mall to shop because of this crime factor, and we wanted to stop this immediately!

I checked with the Manager of the City Shopping Mall, explained what the Chief of Police and I wanted to do, he agreed with our recommendations, and it solved our City Shopping Mall stolen car problem. Here is what the Chief of Police and I decided to do, and the City Shopping Mall Manager helped us implement this plan.

The Manager of the city shopping mall gave the city free office space to have a city Police Office at the Mall. We would have Police Officers there during the day and night, as long as the Mall was open to the public. The Police Office was located where everyone at the City Shopping

Mall could see it, and the Police Officers assigned to work at this location, parked their Police Cars in the public parking areas at the mall so everyone could see these Police vehicles in the City Shopping Mall parking lot.

This new City program, having a City Shopping Mall Police Office, was included in the local newspaper, and citizens both within our city and in neighboring communities also became aware of the city having a New Police Office in our City Shopping Mall.

This scared the auto-theft criminals, since more-and-more of them would get caught if they stole a citizen's personal vehicle, and citizens felt safer driving their personal automobiles in our City Shopping Mall to do their shopping.

This Police Office at our City Shopping Mall was there for many years – and it was a great Police Department program to establish since it was well received by citizens, and everyone knew that it reduced the number of personal auto thefts in our City Shopping Mall.

If other Cities have this problem, I would encourage them to do the same thing, since everyone involved seems to agree with this solution, and auto thefts decreased promptly.

I've personally travelled to other cities throughout our nation, and many city shopping malls in cities throughout America also have a City Police Office located in them, since this is a good thing to do, and it reduces all different kinds of possible crimes that might be committed at a city shopping mall!

The Shopping Mall in Our Towns

Over a decade ago, in a city that I was their City Manager, they had a major regional shopping mall. Citizens from the city that I managed, as well as citizens in neighboring communities, would come to this shopping mall to do their personal and family shopping.

Every couple of months, I would walk around this mall, to see how many store vacancies they had. Over the years, all of the Major Tenants were always there, and there was always about ten to twelve small store vacancies. This small store vacancy factor was typical for several years.

One day, I went to a bookstore at the shopping mall, and wanted to buy a hard-back book, and it had a purchase price of about fifty dollars. I was going to buy it, and then I thought, why don't I go home and check on the internet to see what I would have to pay to purchase this book online.

I went online to a few book purchasing websites, and I found out the following information about this book that I almost purchased at the bookstore at the mall:

– The bookstore at the shopping mall had this book for sale for about fifty dollars,
– On the internet I could buy this book used for much less than it was on sale for at the mall,
– I could even rent this book, and I did not even have to purchase it, if I did not want to,
– The actual online cost of this book was about one-fourth less that I could buy it for at the bookstore at the shopping mall,
– So, I purchased this book online and had it sent to me, and it was sent to me with no shipping charges, and
– I received a major personal savings by purchasing this book from an online website on my personal computer at home.

At the time, I thought that fewer young people were going to our shopping malls, since most of them are shopping online from where they live, and that they don't have to waste hours driving to and from their respective local shopping malls.

Also, many things that people buy are cheaper online, since their online purchasing options have multiple purchasing sources to look at before they decide what to purchase, whatever they are seeking to buy at their local shopping mall.

So, years later, when I went to our local shopping mall to see how things were going, I found the following facts:

- Two of the three Major Tenant stores at the shopping mall were closed, and only one Major Tenant store was left,
- When I counted the number of small store vacancies at the shopping mall, there was over twenty small store vacancies,
- Also, I noticed that there were fewer cars in the shopping mall's parking lot,
- That there were fewer people walking around inside of this shopping mall,
- The fewer people at the shopping mall were older, and many were senior citizens,
- This is because fewer young people are going to our shopping malls, since they are purchasing more things online from their home!

This made me wonder that if shopping malls were changing like ours was, that it would be typical for shopping malls in cities throughout America to be changing, and that my city was only normal in this regard.

My only major thought is that what will take the place of the many Major Tenants at our shopping malls, in the future years, as well as the many smaller stores throughout our shopping mall?

This shopping store vacancy problem still exists, for both the Major Tenants as well as the smaller stores, and there are no answers in sight at the present time.

Only time will tell in the future about how America's city shopping malls change, and how they adapt to the conditions to our nation's online purchasing options – which everyone in our nation nowadays has from their respective homes!

Let's all of us watch this issue, since only time will tell the results of this shopping mall trend!

Immigrants on the West and East Coasts of the United States

When I was growing-up in Southern California, primarily in the City of Los Angeles and the City of San Diego, I noticed the influence of our nation's immigrant population in these areas.

For example, the City of Los Angeles had several immigrant citizen sections that reflected their immigrant population from countries located west of our West Coast. These ethnic neighborhoods include:

- Chinatown,
- Filipino town,

- Little Armenia,
- Koreatown,
- Little Ethiopia, and
- Thai town.

The largest immigrant population, immigrant citizens from Mexico, usually lived in the old downtown areas, where the buildings were small and their rent was cheapest.

Some cities even had smaller Korean or Chinese Main Streets, where these immigrant citizens shad many restaurants, stores, bakeries, and many other ethnic-related shops.

When I relocated to New England, to the State of Connecticut, many neighborhoods in my area had clubs and other organizations to reflect our original immigrant populations, those immigrants that came from those nations that were located east of our East Coast.

These clubs and organizations included the following immigrant groups that were located in central Connecticut. These clubs and organizations were called the:

- Irish Ancient Order of Hibernians (formed 1869),
- French-American Club (formed in 1917),
- German-American Club (formed in 1879),
- Hungarian Community Club (formed 1918),
- North Italian Home Club (formed in 1930),
- Polish National Alliance (formed in 1900),
- Portuguese American Club (formed in 1954).

The original immigrants from these countries to our nation established and came to these clubs and organizations for many years, but their grandchildren usually don't. In recent months, in 2020, one of these buildings was "for rent" and another one was "for sale." Immigrant membership in these clubs and organizations had gone down over the years, and continues to do so.

Downtown Improvements

Downtowns in many of our nation's cities, the place where Main Street is, have deteriorated over the years, and in some cities a large shopping mall was built not-to-far from the City's downtown area.

Public officials should improve their downtown area, and start by improving their Main Street, by considering the following public improvement and service program options:

- In many cities, it would be nice to reconstruct their Main Street, which usually consists of narrowing the street, and widening the adjacent sidewalks.
- Consideration should be given to placing new street lights adjacent to a city's reconstructed Main Street, and also planting appropriate trees along the Main Street.

- New street-related trash cans should be placed on, or near, every corner of a street along a City's Main Street.
- On a City's Main Street, and the downtown area, graffiti should be removed. It should be removed by City employees when on public property, and by the property owner when it is on private property.
- Many cities start downtown Police Walking Patrols and Police Bicycle Patrols, since everyone downtown sees these Police Officers, and this helps to reduce and prevent crime. Frequently more citizens go downtown to shop when such patrols exists, and everyone can see them.
- If a city can provide off-street parking, either through a parking lot or a parking garage, this brings more citizens downtown since it is easier to find a place to park your car. Downtowns are limited in size, and there are many more cars on the road now then there were a few decades ago.
- If there are any brownfield sites in a city's downtown area improvements need to be removed and the ground that they are on needs to be decontaminate and cleaned-up. Frequently, States have Brownfield Development Grants to fund and facilitate such a re-development process.
- If a City can restore rivers and streams in their downtown area this should be great too, since many years ago these downtown waterways were placed in concrete pipes so that land in and around the downtown area could be built upon.
- Some old homes, that have deteriorated over the years, can be purchased by the City, these homes can be removed, and the property that they are on can be used to create neighborhood gardens, small parks, and even used as small parking lots.

The above downtown Main Street reconstruction and improvement options can service to renovate City's Main Street as well as its adjacent downtown area.

This is good since, while large stores go to shopping malls, small stores and shops owned by local citizens can locate on a City's Main Street. It is also nice to get non-profit organizations to relocate to the downtown area, since they serve the public too!

My Books — Past, Present, and Future

During my public service career, I have written numerous books, most of them are edited volumes, since I always like to get state-of-the-art best practices in newly evolving fields related to cities and their governments.

I've listed some examples in each of these categories below. Seems like there is always a new subject/field evolving in local government every few years, whether it be related to a new field, like homeland security, or new programs and services in an existing field, such as economic development or police services.

Early in my city management career I wrote/edited the following volumes:

- *Managing America's Cities,*
- *America's Infrastructure: Problems and Prospects,*

- *Proposition 13: Strategies for Hard Times*
- *Economic Development in Local Government, and*
- *Main Street Renewal*, among other.

During the past few years in my city management career, I wrote/edited the following volumes:

- *Immigration and America's Cities,*
- *Community Renewal through Municipal Investment,*
- *Town and Gown Relations,*
- *Homeland Security: Best Practices for Local Government,*
- *Cities and Sports Stadiums,*
- *The Municipal Budget Crunch,*
- *Main Street Renewal,*
- *The Inner-City: A Handbook for Renewal, and*
- *Cities and Nature,* among others.

During the future, in my academic and consulting career, I will do research and write/edit volumes on the following topics:

- *Climate Change and America's Cities,*
- *School Security and Safety,*
- *Gun Safety Practices,*
- *Local Government Election Practices,*
- *Cybersecurity: Threats and Protection,*
- *Privatization: The Provision of Public Services by the Private Sector,*
- *Senior Citizen Care and Services,*
- *Veteran Citizens Care and Services, and*
- *The Coronavirus: Public Services and Finances.*

From an educational standpoint, my goal in writing/editing books is to educate citizens and their public officials about new subjects that relate to their city government. I also feel that it is best to write articles about best proactic4es in these evolving, timely, and dynamic fields It is also good to search for articles written by other public officials on such topics, since they focus on state-of-the-art evolving best practices in such new emerging fields.

Such books, I believe, will help improve our cities during the coming years!

Work Accomplishments

During my public service career in local government (cities), I talked to many other government professions (state and federal), and students, who have noted that it is a lot easier to notice your work-related accomplishments in a city government, then in higher levels of government – like our state and federal governments.

I thought that this was a good point, since local government, primarily cities, are the closet form of government since it has a focus on your community and the citizens that live in it. Over the years, I would drive back to these cities that I managed, and I could still see the improvements that took place when I was their City Manager.

For example, when I would drive in a downtown area, along a Main Street, I would see my following accomplishments that took place while I was their City Manager:

– In one city I could see a former brownfield site development, where the city received a grant from our state government to clean-up this site, and then it was developed, once the site was clean. Now this site is occupied by a public posit office, that provides jobs to its citizens.

– I helped restore rivers and streams in the City's downtown area, since they were covered a century ago in concreate pipes. The City purchased this property, removed the concrete pipes that the downtown streams flowed in, and emancipated the rivers and streams for all of our citizens to enjoy. Now these waterways flow through a park in the city's downtown area.

– Next to the city's downtown area, the City Council approved funds to build a linear trail next to a river, that included long walk-ways, that were paved, so all of our citizens could enjoy them – families, senior citizens in wheelchairs, citizens walk with crutches, and mothers walking with their children in strollers. It was paved so everyone could use it!

– Some old homes were purchased by the city, and then these houses were demolished, and some of these vacant lots became small parks, with benches in them for citizens, some became community gardens, and a few were given to small neighboring businesses that built small parking lots next to where their business was located – this decreased on-street parking in these neighborhoods.

– It was nice to construct a small playground for young children in a city park. Sometimes these parks had picnic tables, and ballfields and a small playground constructed for young children to enjoy.

– It was nice to see some reconstructed Main Streets, where the street was narrowed, the sidewalks were widened, trees were planted on both sides of the street, and new street lights were placed in the city's downtown area.

– It was also nice to reserve some open-space areas next to public schools, especially in a city's downtown area.

– On a city's Main Street, around the downtown area, there was also virtually no graffiti.

– It was also nice to see downtown Police Walking Patrols and Police Bicycle Patrols, since everyone downtown could see our Police Officers, and this helped to reduce crime in and around our downtown areas. More citizens also came to shop downtown when a city ad such police patrols.

While the City Council approved and funded all of these capital improvement projects, only one of these accomplishments resulted from a new law, and it is explained below.

In order to remove graffiti from buildings in the downtown area, I had the City Council approve a new policy that the City would inform the property owners when there was graffiti on their property. They had two-weeks to remove it, or the City would remove it, repaint the area that the graffiti was on, and that the City would bill the property owner for this service.

Because of this new policy, citizens that had graffiti on their property were notified to remove it, and most of them did. If they did not remove it by the deadline imposed, the City staff would remove it and we would bill the property owner for the cost of this service.

These examples prove that you can get a city's elected officials to approve new programs, such as those described above, have them approve funding for them, and that the City's staff, typically the City Manager working with Department Managers, would implement such programs.

Once these downtown-improvement programs were implemented everyone could see the results – for years to come!

I would encourage young people, and citizens looking to work in government, to choose a local government, primarily cities, for these reasons. You can immediately see the results of your accomplishments, both now and for many years to come.

You can not see such work-related accomplishments in our state or federal governments!

Additional City Resources from Professional Associations and Other Organizations

The people that work for cities are elected, and appointed, and virtually all of them belong to national professional associations. These associations all have websites that have state-of-the-art program information about the best evolving practices in each of these fields.

There are also some other national and international organizations that focus in city governments, and they are also an excellent source of information about state-of-the-art best practices in the various functions of city government, including evolving programs and services. Their organizational websites also have this information on them for citizens to review.

The titles of the elected officials, the titles of city departments, and other national and international organizations are shown below for the reader's information. The names of these professional association and other national and international organizations are shown below, including their respective titles and websites.

Elected Officials:

Mayors
U.S. Conference of Mayors (USCM) (website: www.usmayors.org/)

City Councilors
National League of Cities (NLC) (website: www.nlc.org/)

Appointed by Elected Officials:

City Attorney
International Municipal Lawyers Association (IMLA) (website: www.imla.org/)

City Manager

International City/County Management Association (ICMA) (website: www.icma.org/)

Departments:

Building Department

International Association of Building Officials (IABO) (website: www.iaboinc.org/)

City Clerk Department

International Institute of Municipal Clerks (IIMC) (website: www.iimc.com/)

Finance Department

Government Finance Officers Association (GFOA) (website: www.gfoa.org/)

Fire Department

International Association of Fire Chiefs (IAFC) (website: www.iafc.org/)

Human Resources Management Department

International Personnel Management Association – Human Resources (website: www.ipma-hr.org)

Information Technology Department

Information Technology Management Associate (ITMA) (website: www.itma.net/)

Library Department

American Library Association (ALA) (website: www.ala.org/)

Parks and Recreation Department

National Recreation and Park Association (NRPA) (website: www.nrpa.org/)

Planning Department

American Planning Association (APA) (website: www.planning.org/)

Police Department

International Association of Chiefs of Police (IACP) (website: www.theiacp.org/)

Public Works Department

American Public Works Association (APWA) (website: www.apwa.net/)

Other City Government Organizations:

International Downtown Association (IDA) (website: www.downtown.org/)

International Economic Development Council (IEDC) (website: www.iedconline.org/)

National Association of Towns and Townships (NATaT) (website: www.natat.org/)

National Civic League (NCL) (website: www.national civicleague.org/)

The Urban Institute (TUI) (website: www.urban.org/)

These national and international professional associations make their websites available 24-7 to citizens throughout the world. Anyone can check-out these websites for specific resources, and current and evolving best practices in the fields that they specialize in.

For elected and appointed public officials, they virtually all join these professional associations, and their city government pays for their membership in these organizations. Many of these professional associations have state chapters, hold annual conferences, and monthly meetings, for their respective members.

APPENDICES

A. Glossary of Terms

Following is a list of terms commonly used to describe city, county, regional, state, and federal governments, and the actions taken by their public officials.

Abolish To do away with; to put an end to.

Act Legislation which has passed both Houses of Congress, approved by the President, or passed over his veto thus becoming law. Also used technically for a bill that has been passed by one House and engrossed.

Adjourn To stop or interrupt a meeting or session for a certain length of time.

Amendment A proposal by a member (in committee or floor session of the respective Chamber) to alter the language or provisions of a bill or act. It is voted on in the same manner as a bill.

Appeal A request for a new hearing with a higher court.

Appellate Court A court which has the power to hear appeals and reverse court decisions.

Appointed Officials Public officials appointed by elected officials. These officials typically include an organization's top management staff (that is, chief executive and department managers).

Appointment An office or position for which one is chosen, not elected.

Appropriation A formal approval to draw funds from the Treasury for specific purposes. This may occur through an annual appropriations act, an urgent or supplemental appropriations act, a continuing resolution, or a permanent basis.

At-large Elections An election system where candidates are elected on a city-wide basis.

Authorization A law creating or sustaining a program, delegating power to implement it, and outlining its funding. Following authorization, an appropriation actually draws funds from the Treasury.

Bill A proposed law which is being considered for approval.

Bipartisanship Cooperation between Members of both political parties in addressing a particular issue or proposal. Bipartisan action usually results when party leaders agree that an issue is of sufficient national importance as to preclude normal considerations of partisan advantage.

Board of Supervisors Typical name for the members of the governing body of a county.

Boards and Commissions Typical names given to advisory bodies, appointed by the members of a governing body, to advise them on matters of importance in one of the many functional areas of government.

Calendar A list of bills, resolutions, or other matters to be considered before committees or on the floor of either House of Congress.

Campaign An attempt to convince people to vote for someone for public office.

Candidate A person seeking to obtain an office or position.

Census An official count of the population.

Charter A written grant which establishes a local government corporation or other institution, and defines its purposes and privileges.

Checks and Balances System of government which maintains balance of power among the branches of the government. Sets limits on the power of each branch. Sets up ways for each branch to correct any misuses of power by the other branches.

Citizen Participation Strategies have greater legitimacy and are easer to implement politically when the citizens served by a governmental entity feel that their interests and issues have been properly addressed during the planning process.

City council Typical name for the members of a governing body of a municipality.

City Manager The Chief Executive Officer of a municipality.

Civil Relating to the rights of individuals, such as property and personal freedoms. Also, court cases which are not criminal.

Civil Rights Rights which belong to a person because of his or her being a member of a particular society, for example, an American.

Combination Elections A hybrid election system where some candidates are elected on a city-wide basis, while other candidates are elected from a district, or ward.

Committee A group of people officially chosen to investigate or discuss a particular issue.

Compromise To settle differences by accepting less than what was wanted.

Constraint Limitation; restriction.

Contradict To conflict with; to oppose.

Controversial Relating to issues about which people have and express opposing views.

Cost/Benefit Analysis The relationship between economic benefits and cost associated with the operation of the department or program under study. The cost/benefit analysis may include both direct and indirect benefits and costs. Such analysis typically results in a payback period on initial investment.

Cost Center The smallest practical breakdown of expenditure and income into a grouping which will facilitate performance review, service evaluation, and the setting of priorities for particular activity or service area. Typically, it includes a portion of a single program within a department.

County Manager The Chief Executive Officer of a county government.

Cross-Impact Analysis An analytical technique for identifying the various impacts of specific events or well-defined policy actions on other events. It explores whether the occurrence of one event or implementation of one policy is likely to inhibit, enhance, or have no effect on the occurrence of another event.

Criminal Relating to court cases in which a person has been accused of committing an action that is harmful to the public, such as murder or burglary.

Debate To discuss reasons for and against an issue or idea.

Delegate To grant or assign responsibility to another; to authorize a person or persons to represent the rest of the people.

Direct Democracy The people vote to make all of the decisions about their government.

Discrimination Being treated differently, usually worse, for some characteristic such as race, religion, national origin or sex. Discrimination is discouraged in the U.S.

District Elections An election system where candidates are elected from a district, or ward.

Econometric Model Forecasting technique that involves a system of interdependent regression equations that describe some sector of economic sales or profit activity. The parameters of the regression equations are usually estimated simultaneously. This technique better expresses the casualties involved than an ordinary regression equation.

Effectiveness Performing the right tasks correctly, consistent with a program's mission, goals, and objectives, or work plan. Relates to correctness and accuracy, not the efficiency of the program or tasks performed. Effectiveness alone is not an accurate measure of total productivity.

Efficiency Operating a program or performing work task economically. Relates to dollars spent or saved, not to the effectiveness of the program or task performed. Efficiency alone is not an accurate measure of total productivity.

Elected Officials Those public officials that hold elective office for a specified time period, typically called a term of office.

Environmental Scanning Process of identifying major environmental factors, events, or trends that impact, directly or indirectly, the organization and its internal operating systems. It is one of the initial steps in undertaking a strategic planning process.

Evaluation Systematic review of the mission, goals, objectives, and work plan for the organization and its various components. Evaluation occurs most frequently at the operational level by reviewing organizational objectives. The evaluation process typically results in the preparation of recommendations for needed adjustments.

Executive Person or group of persons responsible for governmental affairs and enforcement of laws.

Executive Director The title frequently used for the Chief Executive Officer of a regional government agency.

Exempt Free or excused from a requirement or duty.

External Environment All relevant elements or forces (for example, social, economic, political, and technological) external to, and having an impact on, the organization and its various components. Includes those forces that are not under the direct control of management.

Forecasting Techniques Methods (for example, qualitative, quantitative, and causal) used to project trends and predict future events or courses of action. Forecasting is an essential component of the strategic planning process. It may be used to analyze the external environment or to project organizational capabilities.

Foreign Policy The way a country treats and relates to the other countries of the world.

Forms of County Government Major forms include Commission, Commission-Administrator, and Council-Executive.

Forms of Municipal Government Major forms include Council-Manager, Mayor-Council, Commission, and Strong Mayor.

General Election A voting process involving most or all areas of the nation or state.

General Purpose Local Governments Includes cities and counties, since they both provide a wide range of services to the citizens they serve.

Gerrymandering Drawing of district lines to maximize the electoral advantage of political party or faction. The term was first used in 1812, when Elbridge Gerry was Governor of Massachusetts, to characterize the State redistricting plan.

Governor The Chief Executive Officer of a state government.

Hierarchical Ordered by rank or authority.

Hierarchy The order in which authority is ranked.

Impeach To charge a public official with committing a crime.

Inaugurate To place in office by a formal ceremony.

Influence The power to produce or cause an effect; to have an effect upon.

Inherent Rights Essential, basic rights.

Intergovernmental Relations The relationships between public officials at the various levels of government, most often dictated by legislation (e.g., grant requirements).

Internal Environment Relevant elements or forces (e.g., personnel, financial, communications, authority relationships, and management operating systems) internal to, and having an impact on, the operation of the organization and its various components. Includes those forces that are under the direct control of management.

Issue Trend, set of elements, or event which a group decides is important for policy-making purposes.

Issues Management Attempt to manage those issues that are important to an organization. These issues typically surface after the completion of an environmental scanning process, or other practice, leading to the identification of important issues. The issues identified should fall within the scope and purpose of the organization.

Jury A group of people chosen to hear a case in court. The *jury* makes a decision based upon the evidence.

Lame Duck Session A session of Congress meeting after elections have been held, but before the newly elected Congress has convened.

Law In municipal and county government this takes the form of an ordinance, which must be passed by majority vote of the governing body and published in a newspaper of general circulation.

Legislation The act or procedure of making laws; a law or laws made by such a procedure.

Levy To collect, a tax, for example.

Life-Cycle Analysis Involves an analysis and forecasting of new product or service growth rates based on S-curves. The phases of product or service acceptance by various groups are central to this analytical technique.

Line Personnel in those departments charged with responsibility for those functions necessary for the day-to-day performance of the organization. Includes those departments that directly produce goods and/or services to satisfy an organization's marketplace.

Line of Succession Order to succession.

Long-Range Planning Includes a planning process that commences with analyzing the internal organization and projecting current trends into the future for selected organizational components. This planning process may not include an assessment of an organization's external environment. It may be product or service oriented. This term should not be confused with strategic planning.

Management Consists basically of two types—strategic and operational. Strategic management is performed at the top of an organization's hierarchy; everything else is operational management. Operational management is organized along functional lines of responsibility. Strategic management sets direction for the organization, and operational management ensures that this direction is implemented.

Management Information System Integrated information system designed to provide strategic, tactical, and operational information to management. Usually involves periodic written or computer-generated reports which are timely, concise, and meaningful.

Management Operating System Formal system of linkages between different components of the organization by which the various departments communicate with each other and by which management directs the operation and receives information on its performance.

Mayor Typical name for the highest elective office in municipality.

Mission Statement of the role, or purpose, by which an organization plans to serve society. Mission statements may be set for different organizational components or departments. A department usually has only one mission statement.

Municipal The smallest unit of local government in the U.S.

Negotiate To discuss and then compromise on an issue to reach an agreement.

Nonprofit Organization Sometimes referred to as the third sector—the other two being the public and private sectors. Nonprofit organizations generally serve a public purpose and do not generate revenues beyond their operating expenses.

Objectives Tasks which are deemed necessary for an organization, or its components and departments, to achieve its goals. Several detailed objectives are typically set forth for each goal statement. Objectives include the operational implementation of goals.

Operational Issues Issues that relate to the internal operations of an organization such as finance, budgeting, personnel, and technology, to name a few. Operational issues may or may not relate to an organization's external environment and may not be of strategic importance to an organization.

Operational Management Tasks performed by line managers dealing with the operations of the organization. Operational managers may provide input into the formulation of strategic plans, but such plans are formulated by the planning group. Operational managers are key actors in implementing components of strategic plans.

Opponent Person who ran against others in an election for an office or position.

Opportunity Cost Cost of not taking a particular course of action. For example, if there are two issues and one is deemed to be strategic and the other is not, then the opportunity cost is the cost of not pursuing the course of action required for the nonstrategic issue. If the purchase of computers is a strategic issue, and the cost to purchase typewriters is not, then the cost of not acquiring the typewriters is an opportunity cost.

Override To nullify; to pass over.

Pardon To forgive a person for something he/she did wrong; to release or free a person from punishment.

Petition A formal request, usually written, for a right or benefit from a person or group with authority.

Philosophy The general beliefs, attitudes and ideas or theories of a person or group.

Platform The stated principles of a candidate for public office or a political party.

Policy Chosen course of action designed to significantly affect the organization's behavior in prescribed situations.

Political Action Committee (PAC) A group organized to promote its members' views on selected issues, usually through raising money that is contributed to the campaign funds of candidates who support the group's position.

President The Chief Executive Officer of the federal government organization.

Productivity Measure of performance that includes the requirements of both efficiency and effectiveness. Includes performing the program or work tasks correctly (effectively) and economically (efficiently).

Pro Tempore For the time being; temporarily.

Preliminary Introductory; something that comes before and is necessary to what follows.

Preside To hold the position of authority; to be in charge of a meeting or group.

Primary Election Election by which the candidate who will represent a particular political party is chosen.

Ratification Two uses of this term are: (1) the act of approval of a proposed constitutional amendment by the legislatures of the States; (2) the Senate process of advice and consent to treaties negotiated by the President.

Ratify To approve or confirm formally; to make valid and binding.

Redistricting The process within the States of redrawing legislative district boundaries to reflect population changes following the decennial census.

Regional Government A multi-jurisdictional agency that includes any combination of cities and counties, and is usually sub-state in nature. Only a few regional governments involve more than one state.

Regulation Rule or order which controls actions and procedures.

Repeal To take back or recall, usually a law.

Representative Democracy The people choose or elect officials to make decisions for them about their government. On some issues, however, the people vote, rather than their representatives.

Republican Democratic; representative.

Resolution A legislative act without the force of law, such as action taken to adopt a policy or to modify an existing program.

Ruling The official decision of a court on the case being tried.

Sentence Judgment or decision; usually a decision on the punishment for a person convicted of a crime.

Special Purpose Local Governments Includes special districts, which perform a single public service or function (e.g., water, sewer, and transportation districts, to name a few).

Staff Personnel in those departments designed to serve the operating components, or line departments, of an organization (e.g., personnel, finance, general services, purchasing, etc.).

Stakeholder Those individuals, groups, and outside parties that either affect or who are affected by the organization. Examples include constituents, special-interest groups, suppliers, unions, employees, policy-makers, and advisory bodies, to name a few. In any strategic planning process these entities must either be involved or consulted so that their views are given consideration during the planning process.

Strategic Issues Issues included in a strategic plan which are deemed important to the organization and its future performance. These issues may be either internal or external to the organization itself. Typically, external issues are more difficult to manage than internal issues, due to the limited degree of control exercised by public organizations over their outside environment.

Strategic Management Involves setting direction for the organization and typically performed by elected and appointed officials, or some combination of these individuals, once a strategic plan is approved for implementation. While the strategic plan is approved by elected officials, top management is responsible for its administrative implementation.

Strategic Vision Explicit, shared understanding of the nature and purpose of the organization. It specifies what the organization is and should be rather than what it does operationally. The strategic vision is contained within an organization's strategy statement.

Strategy General direction set for the organization and its various components to achieve a desired state in the future. Strategy results from the detailed planning process that assesses the external and internal environment of an organization and results in a work plan that includes mission statements to direct the goals and objectives of the organization.

Structure Segmentation of work into components, typically organized around those goods and services produced, the formal lines of authority and communication between these components, and the information that flows between these communication and authority relationships.

Succession Order in which one person follows another in replacing a person in an office or position.

Table To postpone or delay making a decision on an issue or law.

Time Horizon A timespan included in a plan, or planning document, varies depending on the type of plan being developed. Strategic plans typically have a five or ten year, sometimes longer, time horizon. Operational plans, on the other hand, frequently project a three to five-year timespan into the future.

Unconstitutional In conflict with a constitution.

Veto Power of the head of the executive branch to keep a bill from becoming law.

Editor's Note: Some of the above terms were taken from *U.S. Government Structure* (1987), and *Our American Government* (1993), U.S. Government Printing Office, Washington, D.C. copies of these books may be obtained from the U.S. Government Printing Office, P.O. Box 371954, Pittsburgh, Pennsylvania 15250-7954, or may be ordered over the internet from GPO's online bookstore (http://bookstore.gpo.gov).

B. Local Government Historical Document

(Mecklenburg County was the first local government in America to declare its Independence from Great Britain)

The Mecklenburg Resolution[1]
(May 20, 1775)

I.   Resolved: That whosoever directly or indirectly abets, or in any way, form, or manner countenances the unchartered and dangerous invasion of our rights, as claimed by Great Britain, is an enemy to this country–to America–and to the inherent and inalienable rights of man.

II. *Resolved*: That we do hereby declare ourselves a free and independent people; are, and of right ought to be a sovereign and self-governing association, under the control of no power, other than that of our God and the General Government of the Congress: To the maintenance of which Independence was solemnly pledge to each other was our mutual co-operation, our Lives, our Fortunes, and our most Sacred Honor.

III. *Resolved*: That as we acknowledge the existence and control of no law or legal officer, civil or military, within this county, we do hereby ordain and adopt as a rule of life, all, each, and every one of our former laws, wherein, nevertheless, the Crown of Great Britain never can be considered as holding rights, privileges, or authorities therein.

IV. *Resolved*: That all, each, and every Military Officer in this country is hereby reinstated in his former command and authority, he acting to their regulations, and that every Member present of this Delegation, shall henceforth be a Civil Officer, viz: a Justice of the Peace, in the character of a Committee Man, to issue process, hear and determine all matters of controversy, according to said adopted laws, and to preserve Peace, Union, and Harmony in said county, to use every exertion to spread the Love of Country and Fire of Freedom throughout America, until a more general and organized government be established in this Province

ABRAHAM ALEXANDER, *chairman.*
JOHN MCKNITT ALEXANDER, *Secretary*

REFERENCE

1   This declaration of independence (with supplementary set of resolutions establishing a form of government) was adopted (as it is claimed) by a convention of delegates from different sections of Mecklenburg County, which assembled at Charlotte May 20, 1775.

C. United States Voting Rights History

(Year, Legislation, Impact)

1776	*Declaration of Independence*	Right to vote during the colonial and Revolutionary periods is restricted to property owners.
1787	*United States Constitution*	States are given the power to regulate their own voting rights.
1856	*State Legislation*	North Carolina is the last state to remove property ownership as a requirement for voting.
1868	*14th Amendment to the U.S. Constitution*	Citizenship is granted to all former slaves. Voters are still defined as male. Voting regulations are still a right of the states.
1870	*15th Amendment to the U.S. Constitution*	It is now law that the right to vote cannot be denied by the federal or state governments based on race.
1887	*Dawes Act*	Citizenship is granted to Native Americans who give up their Tribal affiliations.
1890	*State Constitution*	Wyoming is admitted to statehood and becomes the first state to legislate voting rights for women in its state constitution.
1913	*17th Amendment to the U.S. Constitution*	New law that allows citizens to vote for members of the U.S. Senate, instead of the past practice of having them elected by State Legislatures.
1915	*U.S. Supreme Court Decision*	The U.S. Supreme Court outlawed, in *Guinn v. United States* (Oklahoma), literacy tests for federal elections. The court ruled that this practice was in violation of the 15th Amendment to the U.S. Constitution.
1920	*19th Amendment to the U.S. Constitution*	Women were given the right to vote in both state and federal elections.
1924	*Indian Citizenship*	This law granted all Native Americans the rights of citizenship, including the right to vote in federal elections.

1944	*U.S. Supreme Court Decision*	The U.S. Supreme Court outlawed, in *Smith v. Alwright* (Texas), "white primaries" in Texas and other States. The court ruled that this practice was in violation of the 15th Amendment to the U.S. Constitution.
1957	*Civil Rights Act*	The first law to implement the 15th Amendment to the U.S. Constitution is passed. This law established the Civil Rights Commission, which formally investigates complaints of voter discrimination made by citizens.
1960	*U.S. Supreme Court Decision*	The U.S. Supreme Court, in *Gomillion v. Lightfoot* (Alabama), outlawed the use of "gerrymandering" in election practices. This practice includes boundary determination (or redistricting) changes being made for electoral advantage.
1961	*23rd Amendment to the U.S. Constitution*	Citizens of Washington, DC, are given the right to vote in presidential elections.
1964	*24th Amendment to the U.S. Constitution*	The right for citizens to vote in federal elections cannot be denied for failure to pay a poll tax.
1965	*Voting Rights Act*	This law forbids states from imposing discriminatory restrictions on the voting rights of citizens, and provides mechanisms to the federal government for the enforcement of this law. This Act was expanded and renewed in 1970, 1975, 1982, and 2006.
1966	*U.S. Supreme Court Decision*	The U.S. Supreme Court, in *Harper v. Virginia Board of Education* (Virginia), eliminated the poll tax as a qualification for voting in any election. This practice was found to be in violation of the 24th Amendment to the U.S. Constitution.
1966	*U.S. Supreme Court Decision*	The U.S. Supreme Court, in *South Carolina v. Katzenbach* upheld the legality of the Voting Rights Act of 1965.
1970	*U.S. Supreme Court Decision*	The U.S. Supreme Court, in *Oregon v. Mitchell* (Oregon), upheld the ban on the use of literacy tests as a requirement for voting. This ban was made permanent in the 1975 Amendments to the Voting Rights Act.
1971	*26th Amendment to the U.S. Constitution*	The national legal voting age is reduced from 21 years old to 18 years old.

1972	*U.S. Supreme Court Decision*	The U.S. Supreme Court, in *Dunn v. Blumstein* (Tennessee), ruled that lengthy residency requirements for voting in state and local elections are unconstitutional, and suggested a 30-day residency period as being adequate.
1975	*Amendments to the Voting Rights Act*	Mandated that certain voting materials must be printed in languages besides English so that people who do not read English can participate in the voting process.
1993	*National Voter Registration Act*	Attempts to increase the number of eligible citizens who register to vote by making registration available at each state's Department of Motor Vehicles, as well as public assistance and disability agencies.
2002	*Help America Vote Act*	Law requires that states comply with federal mandates for provisional ballots; disability access; centralized, computerized voting lists; electronic voting; and the requirement that first-time voters present identification before they can vote.
2003	*Federal Voting Standards And Procedures Act*	Requires all states to streamline their voter registration process, voting practices, and election procedures.

NOTE

For additional information concerning these documents, and related information, please refer to the *Federal Election Commission*, which is listed in the *National Resource Directory* section of this volume.

D. Model City Charter Election Guidelines

Section 6.01. City Elections.

(a) **Regular Elections.** The regular city election shall be held at the time established by state law.

(b) **Registered Voter defined.** All citizens legally registered under the constitution and laws of the state of _____ to vote in the city shall be registered voters of the city within the meaning of this charter.

(c) **Conduct of Elections**. The provisions of the general election laws of the stat of _____ shall apply to elections held under this charter. All elections provided for by the charter shall be conducted by the election authorities established by law. Candidates shall run for office without party designation. For the conduct of city elections, for the prevention of fraud in such elections and for the recount of ballots in cases of doubt or fraud, the city council shall adopt ordinances consistent with law and this charter, and the election authorities may adopt further regulations consistent with law and this charter and the ordinances of the council. Such ordinances and regulations pertaining to elections shall be publicized in the manner of city ordinances generally.

Section 6.02. Council Districts; Adjustment of Districts. (For use with Alternatives II, III and IV of §2.02)

(a) **Number of District.** There shall be _____ city council districts.

(b) **Districting Commission; composition; Appointment; Terms; Vacancies; Compensation.**

   (1) There shall be a districting commission consisting of five members. No more than two commission members may belong to the same political party. The city council hall appoint four members. These four members shall, with the affirmative vote of at least three, choose the fifth member who shall be chairman.

   (2) No member of the commission shall be employed by the city or hold any other elected or appointed position in the city.

   (3) The city council shall appoint the commission no later than one year and five months before the first general election of the city council after each federal decennial census. The commission's term shall end upon adoption of a districting plan, as set forth in §6.02(c)

   (4) In the event of a vacancy on the commission by death, resignation or otherwise, the city council shall appoint a new member enrolled in the same political party from which his or her predecessor was selected, to serve the balance of the term remaining.

   (5) No member of the districting commission shall be removed from office by the city council except for cause and upon notice and hearing.

   (6) The members of the commission shall serve without compensation except that each member shall be allowed actual and necessary expenses to be audited in the same manner as other city charges.

(7) The commission may hire or contract for necessary staff assistance and may require agencies of city government to provide technical assistance. The commission shall have a budget as provided by the city council.

(c) Powers and Duties of the Commission; Hearings, Submissions and Approval of Plan.

(1) Following each decennial census, the commission shall consult the city council and shall consult the city council and shall prepare a plan for dividing the city into districts for the election of council members. In preparing the plan, the commission shall be guided by the criteria set forth in §6.02(d). The report on the plan shall include a map and description of districts recommended.

Reprinted with permission from Model City Charter, 1996. *Published by the National Civic League Press, Denver, Colorado.*

(2) The commission shall hold one or more public hearings not less than one month before it submits the plan to the city council.

(3) The commission shall make its plan available to the public for inspection and comment not less than one month before its public hearing.

(4) The commission shall submit its plan to the city council not less than one year before the first general election of the city council after each decennial census.

(5) The plan shall be deemed and adopted by the city council unless disapproved within three weeks by the vote of the majority of all members of the city council. I the city council fails to adopt the plan, it shall return the plan to the commission with its objections, and with the objections of individual members of the council.

(6) Upon rejection of its plan, the commission shall prepare a revised plan and shall submit such revised plan to the city council no later than nine months before the first general election of the city council after the decennial census. Such revised plan shall be deemed adopted by the city council unless disapproved within two weeks by the vote of two-thirds of all of the members of the city council and unless, by vote of two-thirds of all of its members, the city council votes to file a petition in the_____ Court, _____County, for a determination that the plan fails to meet the requirements of this charter. The city council shall file its petition no later than ten days after it disapproval of the plan. Upon a final determination upon appeal, if any, that the plan meets the requirements of this charter, the plan shall be deemed adopted by the city council and the commission shall deliver the plan to the city clerk. The plan delivered to the city clerk shall include a map and description of the districts.

(7) If in any year population figures are not available at least one year and five months before the first general election following the decennial census, the city council may be local law shorten the periods provided for districting commission action in subsections (2), (3), (4) and (5) of this section.

(d) Districting Plan; Criteria. In preparation of its plan for dividing the city into districts for the election of council members, the commission shall apply the following criteria which, to the extent practicable, shall be applied and given priority in the order in which they are herein set forth

(1) Districts shall be equal in population except where deviations from equality result from the application of the provisions hereinafter set forth, but no such deviation may exceed five percent of the average population for all city council districts according to the figures available from the most recent census.

(2) Districts shall consist of contiguous territory; but land areas separated by waterways shall not be included in the same district unless said waterways are traversed by highway bridges, tunnels or regularly scheduled ferry services both termini of which are within the district, except that, population permitting, islands are not connected to the mainland or to other islands by bridge, tunnel or regular ferry services shall be included in the same district as the nearest land area within the city and, where such subdivisions exist, within the same ward or equivalent subdivision as described in subdivision (5), below.

(3) No city block shall be divided in the formation of districts.

(4) In cities whose territory encompasses more than one county or portions of more than one county, the number of districts which include territory in more than one county shall be as small as possible.

(5) In the establishment of districts within cities whose territory is divided into wards or equivalent subdivisions whose boundaries have remained substantially unaltered for at least fifteen years, the numbers of such wards or equivalent subdivisions whose territory is divided among more than one district shall be as small as possible.

(6) Consistent with the forgoing provisions, the aggregate length of all district boundaries shall be as short as possible.

(e) Effect of Enactment. The new city council districts and boundaries as of the date of enactment shall supersede previous council districts and boundaries for all purposes of the next regular city election, including nominations. The new districts and boundaries shall supersede previous districts and boundaries for all other purposes as of the date on which all council members elected at that regular city election take office

[Section 6.03. Initiative and Referendum.

The powers of initiative and referendum are hereby reserved to the electors of the city. The provisions of the election law of the state of _____, as they currently exist or may hereafter be amended or superseded, shall govern the exercise of the powers of initiative and referendum under this charter.]

Note: Section 6.03 is in brackets because not all states provide for the initiative and referendum and it is possible that not all cities within the state that do provide for it will choose to include the option in their charters.

Commentary on Article VI

In previous editions of the Model detailed provisions on the nomination and election process were included. This edition recognizes that the election laws of each state apply to municipalities whether or not they operate with a local charter. Areas of local discretion are few. Among those discretionary areas may be the provision of nonpartisan elections and the timing of elections. Operating within the limitations imposed by state law, the city may by ordinance adopt regulations deemed desirable.

§6.01. City Elections.

Although in most states local elections are regulated entirely or to a very substantial extent by state statutes, certain variations may be provided by local charter; for example, home rule charters may provide for nonpartisan local elections as provided in this section. When possible, it is particularly desirable to separate municipal from state and national elections. Therefore, municipal elections are frequently scheduled in the fall of odd-numbered years or in the spring of the year – both as a result of state election laws and of city chargers. This separation is important whether elections are conducted on a partisan or nonpartisan basis. It is recommended that such timing be specified in the charter if it is permissible under the state election laws.

§6.02. Council Districts; Adjustment of Districts.

With three of the five alternatives provided for the election of the city council involving districts, the provision for drawing and redrawing district lines assumes particular importance.

This section is a substantial departure from that in the previous editions because of the necessity of complying with such legal mandates as *Baker v. Carr, Avery v. Midland County; Texas*, and the Voting Rights Act and its amendments. Rather than a two-part process with an advisory commission recommending a plan, followed by city council passage of a plan (which might or might not resemble that of the advisory commission), the *Model* provides for a more direct – redistricting by an independent commission. The lead time for redistricting has been expanded to provide sufficient time to resolve some of the increasing number of local government redistricting suits as well as to provide for sufficient time to comply with the requirements of §5 of the Voting Rights Act where that is applicable. In addition, the *Model* provides for ordered, specific criteria for redistricting based on population rather than the "qualified voter" standard of the sixth edition.

The *Model* provides for a bi-partisan commission. Even cities with non-partisan elections may have problems with political parties (either local or national) wanting to dominate the process to achieve advantage. The fact that the four council appointees (or at least three of the four) must be able to agree on the choice of chairman should facilitate the commission being able to work together.

To avoid the conflict of interest created when council members must consider new districts whose lines may materially affect their political futures, the council can neither approve nor veto the result. The council may, however, prevent implementation of the plan if it finds the plan in violation of the charter and files with the courts for such a determination.

The criteria mandated in this section are designed to preclude gerrymandering either to protect or punish incumbents or to prevent particular voting groups from gaining power. The criteria are unquestionably the most important part of the section. It has been suggested that with the proper ordered criteria, the redistricting process is less open to manipulation and flagrant gerrymandering will almost impossible without a clear violation of the mandated criteria. The criteria concerning waterways and islands should be included in charters where appropriate. The exact terminology for election administration subdivisions (e.g., wards or equivalent subdivision) should be adjusted to conform to state law.

There re cities which prefer to have redistricting done by the city council either because of a belief that the redistricting process essential involves a series of political decisions and that attempts to separate the process from the politics is futile and foolish or because redistricting in the past has been satisfactorily accomplished by the city council and that there is no need for change. Where a city opts for redistricting by the city council, the following previsions should be substituted in §6.02, (b) and (c).

(b) Council to Redistrict. Following each decennial census, the city council shall, by ordinance, adjust the boundaries of the city council districts using the criteria set forth in §6.02(e).

(c) Procedures.

(1) The city council shall hold one or more public hearings prior to bringing any proposed plan to a vote. Proposed plans must be available to the public for inspection and comment not less than one month before the first public hearing on said plan. The plan shall include a map and description of the districts recommended.

(2) The city council shall approve a districting plan no later than 10 months (300 days) prior to the first regular city elections following the decennial census.

(a) Failure to Enact Ordinance. If the city council fails to enact a redistricting plan within the required time, the city attorney shall, the following business day, inform the _____Court, _____County, and ask that a special master be appointed to do the redistricting. The special master shall, within 60 days, provide the court with a plan drawn in accordance with the criteria set forth in §6.02(e). That plan shall have the force of law unless the court finds it does not comply with said criteria. The court shall cause an approved plan to go into effect no later than 210 days prior to the first regular city election after the decennial census. The city shall be liable for all reasonable cost incurred by the special master in preparing the plan for the court.

Subsections 6.02(d) and (e) of the Model should be retained, relettered (e) and (f), and the words "city council" substituted for "commission."

§6.02(d) of the substitute language (Failure to Enact Ordinance), is particularly important because it is designed to be an incentive for the council to get redistricting completed on time. Failure to redistrict will not result in just another election with the same old district as was provided in the previous edition. Even the most divided of city councils would probably prefer to get down to the business of compromise than have a special master redistrict for them – and few would want to explain the additional cost of paying someone else to draw up a plan that probably would not be any more satisfactory than their own compromise.

E. Model County Charter Election Guidelines

Section 6.01. County Elections.

(a) **Regular Elections.** The regular county election shall be held at the time established by state law.

(b) **Registered Voter defined.** All citizens legally registered under the constitution and laws of the state of _____to vote in the county shall be registered voters of the county within the meaning of this charter.

(c) **Conduct of Elections.** The provisions of the general election laws of the state of _____ shall apply to elections held under this charter. All elections provided for by the charter shall be conducted by the election authorities established by law. For the conduct of county elections, for the prevention of fraud in such elections and for the recount of ballots in cases of doubt or fraud, the county council shall adopt ordinances consistent with law and this charter, and the election authorities may adopt further regulations consistent with law and this charter and the ordinances of the council. Such ordinances and regulations pertaining to elections shall be publicized in the manner of county ordinances generally.

Section 6.02. Council Districts; Adjustments of Districts. (For use with alternatives II, III and IV of §2.01)

(a) **Number of Districts.** There shall be _____county council districts.

(b) **Districting Commission: Composition; Appointment; Terms; Vacancies; Compensation**

    (1) There shall be a districting commission consisting of five members. No more than two commission members may belong to the same political party. The county council shall appoint four members. These four members shall, with the affirmative vote of at least three, choose the fifth member who shall be chairman.

    (2) No member of the commission shall be employed by the county or any political subdivision of the county, or hold any other elected or appointed position in the county or any political subdivision of the county.

    (3) The county council shall appoint the commission no later than one year and five months before the first general election of the county council after each federal decennial census. The commission's term shall end upon adoption of a districting plan, as set forth in §6.02©.

    (4) In the event of a vacancy on the commission by death, resignation or otherwise, the county council shall appoint a new member enrolled in the same political party from which his or her predecessor was selected, to serve the balance of the term remaining.

    (5) No member of the districting commission shall be removed from office by the county council except for cause and upon notice and hearing.

(6) The members of the commission shall serve without compensation except that each member shall be allowed actual and necessary expenses to be audited in the same manner as other county charges.

(7) The commission may hire or contract for necessary staff assistance and may require agencies of county government to provide technical assistance. The commission shall have a budget as provided by the county council.

(c) Powers and Duties of the Commission; Hearings, Submissions and Approval of Plan.

(1) Following each decennial census, the commission shall consult the county council and shall prepare a plan for dividing the county into districts for the election of council members. In preparing the plan, the commission shall be guided by the criteria set forth in §6.02(d). The report on the plan shall include a map and description of districts recommended.

Reprinted with permission from Model County Charter, 1990. *Published by the National Civic League Press, Denver, Colorado.*

(2) The commission shall hold one or more public hearings not less than one month before it submits the plan to the county council. The commission shall make its plan available to the public for inspection and comment not less than one month before its public hearing.

(3) The commission shall submit its plan to the county council not less than one year before the first general election of this county council after each decennial census.

(4) The plan shall be deemed adopted by the county council unless disapproved within three weeks by the vote of the majority of all members of the county council. If the county council ails to adopt the plan, it shall return the plan to the commission with its objections, and with the objections of individual members of the council.

(5) Upon rejection of its plan, the commission shall prepare a revised plan and shall submit such revised plan to the county council no later than nine months before the first general election of the county council after the decennial census. Such revised plan shall be deemed adopted by the county council unless disapproved within two weeks by the vote of two-thirds of all of the members of the county council and unless, by a vote of two-thirds of all of its members, the county council votes to file a petition in the _____ Court, _____County, for a determination that the plan fails to meet the requirements of this charter. The county council shall file its petition no later than ten days after its disapproval of the plan. Upon a final determination upon appeal, if any, that the plan meets the requirements of this charter, the plan shall be deemed adopted by the county council and the commission shall deliver the plan to the county clerk. The plan delivered to the county clerk shall include a map and description of the districts.

(6) If in any year population figures are not available at least one year and five months before the first general election following the decennial census, the county council may by ordinance shorten the time periods provided for districting commission action in subsections (2), (3), (4) and (5) of this section.

(d) Districting Plan; Criteria. In preparation of its plan for dividing the county into districts for the election of council members, the commission shall apply the following criteria which, to the extent practicable, shall be applied and given priority in the order in which they are herein set forth.

(1) Districts shall be equal in population except where deviations from equality result from the application of the provisions hereinafter set forth, but no such deviation may exceed five percent of the average population for all county council districts according to the figures available from the most recent census.

(2) Districts shall consist of contiguous territory; but land areas separated by waterways are traversed by highway bridges, tunnels or regularly scheduled ferry services both termini of which are within the district, except that, population permitting, islands not connected to the mainland or to other islands by bridge, tunnel or regular ferry services shall be included in the same district as the nearest land area within the county and, where such subdivisions exist, within the same ward or equivalent subdivision as described in subsection (5), below.

(3) No city block shall be divided in the formation of districts.

(4) A municipality within a county shall be divided among as few districts as possible.

(5) In the establishment of districts within counties whose territory is divided into wards or equivalent subdivisions whose boundaries have remained substantially unaltered for at least fifteen years, the number of such wards or equivalent subdivisions whose territory is divided among more than one district shall be as small as possible.

(6) Consistent with the foregoing provisions, the aggregate length of all district boundaries shall be as short as possible.

(e) Effect of Enactment. The new county council districts and boundaries as of the date of enactment shall supersede previous council districts and boundaries for all purposes of the next regular county election, including nominations. The new districts and boundaries shall supersede previous districts and boundaries for all other purposes as of the date on which all council members elected at that regular county election take office.

[Section 6.03. Initiative and Referendum

The powers of initiative and referendum are hereby reserved to the electors of the county. The provisions of the election law of the state of _____, as they currently exist or may hereby be amended or superseded, shall govern the exercise of the powers of initiative and referendum under this charter.]

Note: Section 6.03 is in brackets because not all states provide for the initiative and referendum and it is possible that not all counties within the states that do provide for it will choose to include the option in their charters.

Commentary on Article VI

In previous League models, detailed provisions on the nomination and election process were included. This edition recognizes that the election laws of each state apply to counties whether or not they operate with a local charter. Areas of local discretion are few. Among those discretionary areas may be the provision of nonpartisan elections and the timing of elections. Operating within the limitations imposed by state law, the county may by ordinance adopt regulations deemed desirable.

§6.01. County Elections.

Although in most states local elections are regulated entirely or to a very substantial extent by state statutes, certain variations may be provided by local charter; for example, home rule charters may provide for nonpartisan local elections. When possible, it is particularly desirable to separate local from state and national elections. Therefore, local elections are frequently scheduled in the fall of odd-numbered years or in the spring of the year – both as a result of state election laws and of city and county charters. It is recommended that such timing be specified in the charter if it is permissible under the state election laws.

§6.02. Council Districts; Adjustment of Districts.

With three of the five alternatives provided for the election of the county council involving districts, the provision for drawing and redrawing district lines assumes particular importance.

This section is a substantial departure from that in the previous editions because of the need to comply with such legal mandates as *Baker v. Carr, Avery v. Midland County, Texas*, and the Voting Rights Act and its amendments. Rather than a two-part process with an advisory commission recommending a plan, followed by county council passage of a plan (which might or might not resemble that of the advisory commission), the *Model* provides for a more direct process – redistricting by an independent commission. The lead time for redistricting has been expanded to provide sufficient time to resolve some of the increasing number of local government redistricting suits as well as to provide for sufficient time to comply with the requirements of §5 of the Voting Rights Act where that is applicable. In addition, the *Model* provides for ordered, specific criteria for redistricting based on population.

The *Model* provides for a bi-partisan commission. The fact that the four council appointees (or at least three of the four) must be able to agree on the choice of chairman should facilitate the commission being able to work together.

To avoid the conflict of interest created when councilmembers must consider new districts whose lines may materially affect their political futures, the council can neither approve nor veto the result. The council may, however, prevent implementation of the plan if it finds the plan in violation of the charter and files with the courts for such a determination.

The criteria mandated in this section are designed to preclude gerrymandering either to protect or punish incumbents or to prevent particular voting groups from gaining power. The criteria are unquestionably the most important part of the section. It has been suggested that with the proper ordered criteria, the redistricting process is less open to manipulation and flagrant gerrymandering will be almost impossible without a clear violation of the mandated criteria. The criteria concerning waterways and islands should be included in charters where appropriate. The exact terminology for election administration subdivision (e.g., wards or equivalent subdivisions) should be adjusted to conform to state law.

There are counties which prefer to have redistricting done by the county council either because of a belief that the redistricting process essentially involves a series of political decisions and that attempts to separate the process from the politics is futile and foolish or because redistricting in the past has been satisfactorily accomplished by the council and that there is no need for change. Where a county opts for redistricting by the council, the following provisions should be substituted in §6.02(e).

(b) Council to Redistrict. Following each decennial census, the county council shall, by ordinance, adjust the boundaries of the county council districts using the criteria set forth in §6.02(e).

(c) Procedures.

(1) The county council shall hold one or more public hearings prior to bringing any proposed plan to a vote. Proposed plans must be available to the public for inspection and comment not less than one month before the first public hearing on said plan. The plan shall include a map and description of the districts recommended.

(2) The county council shall approve a districting plan no later than 10 months (300 days) prior to the first regular county election following the decennial census.

(d) Failure to Enact Ordinance. If the county council fails to enact a redistricting plan within the required time, the county attorney shall, the following business day, inform the _____ Court, _____ County, and ask that a special master be appointed to do the redistricting. The special master shall, within 60 days, provide the court with a plan drawn in accordance with the criteria set forth in §6.02(e). That plan shall have the force of law unless the court finds it does not comply with said criteria. The court shall cause an approved plan to go into effect no later than 210 days prior to the first regular county election after the decennial census. The county shall be liable for all reasonable costs incurred by the special master in preparing the plan for the court.

Subsections 6.02(d) and (e) of the *Model* should be retained, relettered (e) and (f), and the words "county council" substituted for "commission."

§6.02(d) of the substitute language (*Failure to Enact Ordinance*), is particularly important because it is designed to be an incentive for the council to get redistricting completed on time. Failure to redistrict will not result in just another election with the same old districts as was provided in the previous edition. Even the most divided of councils would probably prefer to get down to the business of compromise than have a special master redistrict for them – and few would want to explain the additional cost of paying someone else to draw up a plan that probably would not be any more satisfactory than their own compromise.

F. National Resource Directory

(Organized by topics for the public, nonprofit, and educational sectors)

Civic Education

Ackerman Center for Democratic Citizenship
(http://www.education.purdue.edu/ackerman-center)

American Democracy Project
(http://www.aascu.org/programs/adp/)

Bill of Rights Institute
(https://www.billofrightsinstitute.org/)

Center for Civic Education
(http://www.civiced.org/)

Civic Education Project
(http://www.civiceducationproject.org/)

Constitutional Rights Foundation
(http://www.crf-usa.org/)

Kellogg Foundation
(http://www.wkkf.org/)

Civic Renewal Initiative
(http:// ncoc.org/civic-renewal-initiative/)

National Endowment for Democracy
(http://www.ned.org/)

National Institute for Citizens Education and Law
(https://eric.ed.gov)

Civil Rights and Civil Liberties

American Civil Liberties Union
(http://www.aclu.org/)

Constitution Society
(http://www.constitution.org/)

Freedom Forum
(http://www.freedomforum.org/)

League of Women Voters
(http://www.lwv.org/)

National Coalition again Censorship
(http://www.ncac.org/)

Project Vote Smart
(http://www.vote-smart.org/)

Historical

Center for the Study of Federalism
(https://www.federalism.org/)

Center for the Study of the Presidency
(http://www.thepresidency.org/)

Constitutional Facts
(http://www.constitutionfacts.com/)

Freedom Foundation at Valley Forge
(http://www.ffvf.org/)

National Constitution Center
(http://www.constitutioncenter.org/)

Supreme Court Historical Society
(http://www.supremecourthistory.org/)

The Avalon Project
(http://avalon.law.yale.edu/)

White House Historical Association
(http://www.whitehousehistory.org/)

Political Parties

Democratic National Committee
(http://www.democrats.org/)

Green Party of the United States
(https://www.gp.org/)

Libertarian Party
(http://www.lp.org/)

Reform Party
(http://www.reformparty.org/)

Republican National Committee
(http://www.gop.com/)

Socialist Party
(http://www.socialist.org/)

Professional Associations

American Bar Association
(http://www.abanet.org/)

American Planning Association
(http://www.planning.org/)

American Political Science Association
(http://www.apsanet.org/)

American Society for Public Administration
(http://www.aspanet.org/)

Association for Metropolitan Planning
Organizations
(http://www.ampo.org/)

Public Policy

Association for Public Policy Analysis and
Management
(http://www.appam.org/)

Center for Policy Alternatives
(https://www.ncpa.org/)

Center for Public Integrity
(http://www.publicintegrity.org/)

Common Cause
(http://www.commoncause.org/)

National Center for Policy Analysis
(http://www.ncpa.org/)

National Center for Public Policy Research
(http://www.nationalcenter.org/)

National Legal Center for Public Interest
(http://www.nlcpi.org/)

Pew Research Center
(http://pewresearch.org/)

State and Local Government

Council of State Governments
(http://www.csg.org/)

International City/County Management
Association
(http://www.icma.org/)

Local Government Commission
(http://www.lgc.org/)

Meyner Center for the study of State and
Local Government
(https://meynercenter.lafayette.edu/)

National Association of Counties
(http://www.naco.org/)

National Association of Regional Councils
(http://www.narc.org/)

National Association of Towns and Townships
(http://natat.org/)

National Center for State Courts
(http://www.ncsc.org/)

National Civic League
(http://www.ncl.org/)

National Conference of State Legislatures
(http://www.ncsl.org/)

National Governors Association
(http://www.nga.org/)

National League of Cities
(http://www.nlc.org/)

Secretary of State/State of Connecticut
(http://www.sots.ct.gov/)

U.S. Conference of Mayors
(http://www.usmayors.org/)

State Supreme Judicial Court
Commonwealth of Massachusetts
(http://ww.mas.gov/courts/sjc)

U.S. Government
Federal Communications Commission
(http://www.fcc.gov/)

Federal Elections Commission
(http://www.fec.gov/)

Federal Judicial Center
(http://www.fjc.gov/)

Federal Judiciary Homepage
(http://www.uscourts.gov/)

Library of Congress
(http://lcweb.loc.gov/)

National Endowment for the Humanities
(http://www.neh.gov/)

Thomas Legislative Information
(http://www.congress.gov/)

U.S. Census Bureau
(http://www.census.gov/)

U.S. Department of State
(http://www.state.gov)

U.S. Department of the Interior
(http://www.doi.gov/)

U.S. House of Representatives
(http://www.house.gov/)

U.S. National Archives and Records
Administration
(http://www.archives.gov/)

U.S. Senate
(http://www.senate.gov/)

U.S. Supreme Court
(http://www.supremecourtus.gov/)

White House
(http://www.whitehouse.gov/)

Others

Brookings Institution
(http://www.Brookings.edu/)

Civics & The Future of Democracy
(http://futureofcivics.theatlantic.com)

Heritage Foundation
(http://www.heritage.org/)

National Humanities Center
(http://www.nhinet.org/)

National Taxpayers Union
(http://www.ntu.org/)

National Urban League
(http://www.nul.org/)

Smithsonian Institution
(http://www.si.edu/)

Street Law, Inc.
(http://www.streetlaw.org/)

Supreme Court Decisions
(http://law.cornell.edu/supremecourt/)

United Kingdom Parliamentary Archives
(https://www.parliament.uk/archives/)

Urban Institute
(http://www.urban.org/)

Wikipedia Encyclopedia
(http://www.wikipedia.org/)

NOTE

Some professional association are listed under headings that fit their primary mission. Those that don't fit into one of the general topics are listed above under "others."

G. State Municipal League Directory

Most states have a municipal league, which serves as a valuable source of information about city government innovations and programs. Additional information on eminent domain is available from the following state municipal league websites:

Alabama League of Municipalities
(http://www.alalm.org/)

Alaska Municipal League
(http://www.akml.org/)

League of Arizona Cities and Towns
(https://www.azleague.org/)

Arkansas Municipal league
(http://www.arml.org/)

League of California Cities
(http://www.calcities.org/)

Colorado Municipal League
(https://www.cml.org/)

Connecticut Conference of Municipalities
(https://www.ccm-ct.org/)

Delaware League of Local Governments
(https://dllg.delaware.gov)

Florida League of Cities
(https://www.flcities.com)

Georgia Municipal Association
(https://www.gacities.com)

Association of Idaho Cities
(http://www.idahocities.org/)

Illinois Municipal League
(http://www.iml.org/)

Indiana Association of Cities and Towns
(https://aimindiana.org/)

Iowa League of Cities
(http://www.iowaleague.org/)

League of Kansas Municipalities
(http://www.lkm.org/)

Kentucky League of Cities, Inc.
(http://www.klc.org/)

Louisiana Municipal Association
(http://www.lma.org/)

Maine Municipal Association
(http://www.memun.org/)

Maryland Municipal League
(http://www.mdmunicipal.org/)

Massachusetts Municipal Association
(http://www.mma.org/)

Michigan Municipal League
(https://www.mml.org/)

League of Minnesota Cities
(http://www.lmc.org/)

Mississippi Municipal League
(http://www.mmlonline.com/)

Missouri Municipal League
(http://www.mocities.com/)

Montana League of Cities and Towns
(https://mtleague.org)

League of Nebraska Municipalities
(http://www.lonm.org/)

Nevada League of Cities and Municipalities
(http://www.nvleague.org/)

New Hampshire Municipal Association
(http://www.nhmunicipal.org/)

New Jersey State League of Municipalities
(http://www.njlm.org/)

New Mexico Municipal League
(www.nmml.org/)

New York State Conference of Mayors
and Municipal Officials
(http://www.nycom.org/)

North Carolina League of Municipalities
(http://www.nclm.org/)

North Dakota League of Cities
(https://www.ndlc.org/)

Ohio Municipal League
(http://www.omlohio.org/)

Oklahoma Municipal League
(http://www.oml.org/)

League of Oregon Cities
(http://www.orcities.org/)

Pennsylvania Municipal League
(http://www.pml.org/)

Rhode Island League of Cities
And Towns
(http://www.rileague.org/)

Municipal Association of South Carolina
(http://www.masc.sc/)

South Dakota Municipal League
(http://www.sdmunicipalleague.org/)

Tennessee Municipal League
(http://tml1.org/)

Texas Municipal League
(http://www.tml.org/)

Utah League of Cities and Towns
(http://www.ulct.org/)

Vermont League of Cities and Towns
(http://www.vlct.org/)

Virginia Municipal League
(http://www.vml.org/)

Association of Washington Cities
(https://www.wacities.org)

West Virginia Municipal League
(http://www.wvml.org/)

League of Wisconsin Municipalities
(https://www.lwm-info.org/)

Wyoming Association of Municipalities
(http://www.wyomuni.org/)

H. State Library Directory

Most state libraries have copies of state laws, both proposed and adopted in an on-line database. Many states also have copies of the various laws adopted in those cities and towns within their jurisdictions. They are an excellent resource for eminent domain.

Alabama
Alabama Department of Archives &
History,
(http://archives.state.al.us/)

Alabama Public Library Services
(http://statelibrary.alabama.gov/)

Alaska
Alaska State Library
(http://www.library.alaska.gov/)

Arizona
Arizona Department of Library, Archives
and Public Records
(http://www.azlibrary.gov/)

Arkansas
Arkansas State Library
(http://www.asl.lib.ar.us/)

California
California State Library
(http://www.library.ca.gov/)

Colorado
Colorado State Library and Adult
Education Office
(http://www.cde.state.co.us/cdelib/)

Colorado Virtual Library
(http://www.coloradovirtuallibrary.org/)

Connecticut
Connecticut State Library
(http://www.ctstatelibrary.org/)

Delaware
Delaware Library Catalog Consortium
(https://lib.de.us/about-us/about-dlc/)

Delaware Division of Libraries
(http://www.libraries.delaware.gov/)

District of Columbia
District of Columbia Public Library
(http://www.dclibrary.org/)

Florida
State Library and Archives of Florida
(http://www.dos.myflorida.com/library-archives)

Georgia
Office of Public Library Services
(http://www.georgialibraries.org/)

Hawaii
Hawaii State Public Library System
(http://www.librarieshawaii.org/)

Idaho
Idaho Commission for Libraries
(http://libraries.idaho.gov/)

Illinois
Illinois State Library
(http://www.cyberdriveillinois.com/departments/library)

Indiana
Indiana State Library
(http://www.in.gov/library/)

Iowa
State Library of Iowa
(http://www.statelibraryofiowa.org/)

Kansas
Kansas State Library
(http://www.kslib.info/)

Kentucky
Kentucky Department for Libraries and Archives
(http://www.kdla.ky.gov/)

Louisiana
State Library of Louisiana
(http://www.state.lib.la.us/)

Maine
Maine State Library
(http://www.state.me.us/msl.)

Maryland
Sailor: Maryland's Public Information Network
(http://www.sailor.lib.md.us/)

Massachusetts
Massachusetts Board of Library Commissioners
(http://mblc.state.ma.us/)

Michigan
Library of Michigan
(http://www.michigan.gov/libraryofmichigan)

Minnesota
State Government Libraries
(http://www.libraries.state.mn.us/)

Mississippi
Mississippi Library Commission
(http://www.mlc.lib.ms.us/)

Missouri
Missouri State Library
(http://www.sos.mo.gov/library/)

Montana
Montana State Library
(http://www.home.msl.mt.gov/)

Nebraska
Nebraska Library Commission
(http://www.nlc.state.ne.us/)

Nevada
Nevada State Library and Archives
(http://www.nsladigitalcollections.org)

New Hampshire
New Hampshire State Library
(http://www.nh.gov/nhsl/)

New Jersey
The New Jersey State Library
(http://www.njstatelib.org/)

New Mexico
New Mexico State Library
(http://www.nmstatelibrary.org/)

New York
The New York State Library
(http://www.nysl.nysed.gov/)

New York State Archives
(http://www.archives.nysed.gov/)
North Carolina
State Library of North Carolina
(https://statelibrary.ncdcr.gov/)

North Dakota
North Dakota State Library
(http://www.library.nd.gov/)

Ohio
State Library of Ohio
(http://www.library.ohio.gov/)

Oklahoma
Oklahoma Department of Libraries
(http://www.odl.state.ok.us/)

Oregon
Oregon State Library
(http://oregon.gov/OSL/)

Pennsylvania
State Library of Pennsylvania
(https://www.statelibrary.pa.gov/)

Rhode Island
Office of Library and Information Services
(http://www.olis.ri.gov/)

South Carolina
South Carolina State Library
(http://www.statelibrary.sc.gov/)

South Dakota
South Dakota State Library
(http://library.sd.gov/)

Tennessee
Tennessee State Library & Archives
(http://www.tennessee.gov/tsla/)

Texas
Texas State Library and Archives Commission
(http://www.tsl.state.tx.us/)

Utah
Utah State Library
(http://library.utah.gov/libraries.vermont.gov/)

Vermont
Vermont Department of Libraries
(http://libraries.vermont.gov/)

Virginia
The Library of Virginia
(http://www.lva.virginia.gov/)

Washington
Washington State Library
(http://www.secstate.wa.gov/library/)

West Virginia
West Virginia Library Commission
(http://wvlc.lib.wv.us/)

West Virginia Archives and History
(http://www.wvculture.org/history/

Wisconsin
Wisconsin Department of Public Instruction:
Division for Libraries, Technology, and
Community Learning
(http://www.dpi.wi.gov/dltcl/)

Wyoming
Wyoming State Library
(http://www.library.wyo.gov/)

I. Books by Roger L. Kemp

(As author, contributing author, and editor)

(1) Roger L Kemp, *Coping with Proposition 13*, Lexington Books, D.C. Heath and Company, Lexington, MA, and Toronto, Canada (1980)

(2) Roger L. Kemp, "The Administration of Scarcity: Managing Government in Hard Times," *Conferencia De Las Grandes Ciudades De Las America*, Interamerican Foundation of Cities, San Juan, Puerto Rico (1983)

(3) Roger L. Kemp, *Cutback Management: A trinational Perspective*, Transaction Books, New Brunswick, NJ, and London, England (1983)

(4) Roger L. Kemp, *Research in Urban Policy: Coping with Urban Austerity*, JAI Press, Inc., Greenwich, CT, and London, England (1985)

(5) Roger L. Kemp, *America's Infrastructure: Problems and Prospects*, The Interstate Printers and Publishers, Danville, IL (1986)

(6) Roger L. Kemp, *Coping with Proposition 13: Strategies for Hard Times*, Robert E. Krieger Publishing Company, Malabar, FL (1988)

(7) Roger L. Kemp, *America's Cities: Strategic Planning for the Future*, The Interstate Printers and Publishers, Danville, IL (1988)

(8) Roger L. Kemp, *The Hidden Wealth of Cities: Policy and Productivity Methods for American Local Governments,* JAI Press, Inc., Greenwich, CT and London, England (1989*)*

(9) Roger L. Kemp, *Strategic Planning in Local Government: A Casebook*, Planners Press, American Planning Association, Chicago, IL, and Washington, D.C. (1992)

(10) Roger L. Kemp, *Strategic Planning for Local Government*, International City/County Management Association, Washington, D.C. (1993)

(11) Roger L. Kemp, *America's Cities: Problems and Prospects*, Avebury Press, Alershot, England (1995)

(12) Roger L. Kemp, *Helping Business – The Library's Role in Community Economic Development, A How-To-D-It Manual*, Neal-Schuman Publishers, Inc., New York, NY, and London, England (1997)

(13) Roger L. Kemp, *Homeland Security: Best Practices for Local Government*, 1st Edition, International City/County Management Association, Washington, D.C. (2003)

(14) Roger L Kemp, *Cities and the Arts: A handbook for Renewal*, McFarland & Company, Inc., Jefferson, NC (2004)

(15) Roger L. Kemp, *Homeland Security Handbook for Citizen and Public Officials*, McFarland & Company, Inc., Jefferson, NC (2006)

(16) Roger L. Kemp, *Main Street Renewal: A Handbook for Citizens and Public Officials*, McFarland & Company, Inc., Jefferson, NC (2006, 2000)

(17) Roger L. Kemp, *Local Government Election Practices: A Handbook for Public Officials and Citizens*, McFarland & Company, Inc., Jefferson, NC (2006, 1999)

(18) Roger L. Kemp, *Cities and Nature: A Handbook for Renewal*, McFarland & Company, Inc., Jefferson, NC (2006)

(19) Roger L. Kemp, *Emergency Management and Homeland Security*, International City/County Management Association, Washington, D.C. (2006)

(20) Roger L. Kemp, *The Inner City: A Handbook for Renewal*, McFarland & Company, Inc., Jefferson, NC (2007, 2001)

(21) Roger L. Kemp, *Privatization: The Provision of Public Services by the Private Sector,* McFarland & Company, Inc., Jefferson, NC (2007, 1991)

(22) Roger L. Kemp, *Community Renewal through Municipal Investment: A Handbook for Citizens and Public Officials*, McFarland & Company, Inc., Jefferson, NC (2007, 2003)

(23) Roger L. Kemp, *How American Government Works: A Handbook on City, County, Regional, State, and Federal Operations*, McFarland & Company, Inc., Jefferson, NC (2007, 2002)

(24) Roger L. Kemp, *Regional Government Innovations: A Handbook for Citizens and Public Officials*, McFarland & Company, Inc., Jefferson, NC (2007, 2003)

(25) Roger L. Kemp, *Economic Development in Local Government: A Handbook for Public Officials and Citizens*, McFarland & Company, Inc.., Jefferson, NC (2007, 1995)

(26) Roger L. Kemp, *Model Practices for Municipal Governments,* Connecticut Town and City Management Association, University of Connecticut, West Hartford, CT (2007)

(27) Roger L. Kemp, *Managing America's Cities: A Handbook for Local Government Productivity*, McFarland & Company, Inc., Jefferson, NC (2007, 1998)

(28) Roger L. Kemp, *Model Government Charters: A City, County, Regional, State, and Federal Handbook*, McFarland & Company, Inc., Jefferson, NC (2007, 2003)

(29) Roger L. Kemp, *Forms of Local Government: A Handbook on City, County and Regional Options*, McFarland & Company, Inc., Jefferson, NC (2007, 1999)

(30) Roger L. Kemp, *Cities and Cars: A Handbook of Best Practices*, McFarland & Company, Inc., Jefferson, NC (2007)

(31) Roger L. Kemp, *Homeland Security for the Private Sector: A Handbook*, McFarland & Company, Inc., Jefferson, NC (2007)

(32) Roger L. Kemp, *Strategic Planning for Local Government: A Handbook for Officials and Citizens*, McFarland & Company, Inc., Jefferson, NC (2008, 1993)

(33) Roger L. Kemp, *Museums, Libraries and Urban Vitality: A Handbook*, McFarland & Company, Inc., Jefferson, NC (2008)

(34) Roger L. Kemp, *Cities and Growth: A Policy Handbook*, McFarland & Company, Inc., Jefferson, NC (2008)

(35) Roger L. Kemp, *Cities and Sports Stadiums: A Planning Handbook*, McFarland & Company, Inc., Jefferson, NC (2009)

(36) Roger L. Kemp, *Cities and Water: A Handbook for Planning*, McFarland & Company, Inc., Jefferson, NC (2009)

(37) Roger L. Kemp, *Homeland Security: Best Practices for Local Government*, 2nd Edition, International city/County Management Association, Washington, D.C. (2010)

(38) Roger L. Kemp, ***Cities and Adult Businesses: A Handbook for Regulatory Planning***, McFarland & Company, Inc., Jefferson, NC (2010)

(39) Roger L. Kemp, ***Documents of American Democracy: A Collection of Essential Works***, McFarland & Company, Inc., Jefferson, NC (2010)

(40) Roger L. Kemp, ***Strategies and Technologies for a Sustainable Future***, World Future Society, Bethesda, MD (2010)

(41) Roger L. Kemp, ***Cities Going Green: A Handbook of Best Practices,*** McFarland & Company, Inc., Jefferson, NC (2011)

(42) Roger L. Kemp, ***The Municipal Budget Crunch: A Handbook for Professionals***, McFarland & Company, Inc., Jefferson, NC (2012)

(43) Roger L. Kemp, Frank B. Connolly, and Philip K. Schenck, ***Local Government in Connecticut***, 3rd Edition, Wesleyan University Press, Middletown, CT (2013)

(44) Roger L. Kemp, ***Town and Gown Relations: A Handbook of Best Practices***, McFarland & Company, Inc., Jefferson, NC (2013)

(45) Roger L. Kemp, ***Global Models of Urban Planning: Best Practices Outside the United States,*** McFarland & Company, Inc., Jefferson, NC (2013)

(46) Roger L. Kemp, ***Urban Transportation Innovations Worldwide: A Handbook of Best Practices Outside the United States***, McFarland & Company, Inc., Jefferson, NC (2015)

(47) Roger L. Kemp, ***Immigration and America's Cities: A Handbook on Evolving Services***, McFarland & Company, Inc., Jefferson, NC (2016)

(48) Roger L. Kemp, ***Corruption and American Cities: Essays and Case Studies in Ethical Accountability***, McFarland & Company, Jefferson, NC (2016)

(49) Roger L. Kemp, ***Privatization in Practice: Reports on Trends, Cases and Debates in Public Service by Business and Nonprofits***, McFarland & Company, Inc., Jefferson, NC (2016)

(50) Roger L. Kemp, ***Small Town Economic Development: Reports on Growth Strategies in Practice***, McFarland & Company, Inc., Jefferson, NC (2017)

(51) Roger L. Kemp, Donald F. Norris, Laura Mateczun, Cory Fleming, and Will Fricke, ***Cybersecurity: Protecting Local Government Digital Resources***, International City/County Management Association, Washington, D.C. (2017)

(52) Roger L. Kemp, ***Eminent Domain and Economic Growth: Perspectives on Benefits, Harms and Trends***, McFarland & Company, Inc., Jefferson, NC (2018)

(53) Roger L. Kemp, ***Senior Care and Services: Essays and Case Studies on Practices, Innovations and Challenges***, McFarland & Company, Inc., Jefferson, NC (2019)

(54) Roger L. Kemp, ***Cybersecurity: Current Writings on Threats and Protection,*** McFarland & Company, Inc., Jefferson, NC (2019)

(55) Roger L. Kemp, ***Veteran Care and Services: Essays and Case Studies on Practices, Innovations and Challenges,*** McFarland & Company, Inc., Jefferson, NC (2020)

(56) Roger L. Kemp, ***Civics 101- Poems About America's Cities***, Kindle Direct Publishing, Middletown, DE (2020)

(57) Roger L. Kemp, ***Civics 102 – Stories About America's Cities***, Kindle Direct Publishing, Middletown, DE (2020)

J. World Travels by Roger L. Kemp

Roger has visited the following countries, and major geographic regions, throughout the world during his public service and consulting career:

Australia*
Austria
Belgium
Brunei Darussalam
Canada
China
Czech Republic
Fiji
France*
French Polynesia*
Germany*
Hong Kong*
Hungary
Iceland
Indonesia*
Italy*
Japan*
Luxembourg*
Macau
Malaysia*
Mexico
Netherlands
New Zealand*
Philippines*
Puerto Rico*
Singapore*
Slovak Republic
South Korea*
Switzerland
Tahiti*
Thailand
United Kingdom*
United States (all regions, and most states) *
Virgin Islands

*During his visits to many of these locations, Dr. Kemp has met with elected officials, such as a city's Mayor, administrative officers, and department managers. He has also given presentations at several international professional conferences in some of these nations.

K. Some Final Thoughts

Thoughts About America's Cities

El Condor Pasa (If I Could)

I'd rather be a forest than a street.
Yes, I would, If I could, I surely would.

I'd rather feel the earth beneath my feet.
Yes, I would, If I only could, I surely would.

Simon and Garfunkel, 1970

——

<u>America's Livable Cities</u>

Our cities were not designed by city planners,
But by cars, to make the vehicle roadways
And parking spaces available for them.

Our cities must be redesigned by city planners,
To enhance the level of nature within them,
For everyone, especially the citizens who live in our cities.

Roger L. Kemp, 2020

INDEX

A

Accommodating the Homeless 80

Accomplishments, Work 108

Acknowledgements xi

Additional City Resources from Professional
     Associations and Other Organizations 110

America's Cities xiii, xv, xvii, 13, 66, 107, 108, 156,
     157, 158, 160

Appendices xv, 113

Applying for a Job in a Wealthy Community 24

Appointed Officials xi, xiv, 16, 21, 67, 115, 123

Appointment Process, Chief of Police 59

Approval Process, The City Council Budget 46

Audit, Employee Health Benefits 78

Avoiding Vehicle Taxes 89

B

Balance The Budget, Mayor's Request to 45

Balancing a City's Annual Budget 47

Base, Police Access to a Military 36

Being Stopped by the Police – Red Light 67

Being Stopped by the Police – Speeding 41

Benefits Audit, Employee Health 78

The Best Way to Hire Department Managers 27

Books by Roger L. Kemp 156

Budget Approval Process, The City Council 46

Budget, Balancing a City's Annual 47

Budget, Mayor's Request to Balance The 45

Budget Reductions, Possible xiv, 48

Budget Request, Citizen 49

C

Called, A Police Officer 67

Centralized City Purchasing 102

Central Park, The Size of 95

Change Over Time, City Politics xv, 99

Change Over Time, Departmental Services xiv, 73

Charges Against the Chief of Police 60

Charter Oak State College xi

The Chief of Police and the Police Commission 59

Chief of Police Appointment Process xiv, 59

The Chief of Police Appointment Process xiv, 59

Chief of Police, Request from the 62

Cities
     annual budget xiv, 23, 45, 46, 47, 49, 53, 70,
          79, 87
     that the author has lived and worked in xiii
     job opportunities and desired locations 6
     property tax rates xiv, 49
     with large minority populations 33

Cities That I lived and Worked In 5

Citizen Budget Request 49

Citizen Complaints About Employees 34

Citizen Complaints, Processing 81

Citizen Request to Hold Down Property Taxes 87

Citizens, Gifts from 41

Citizens Use of Public Property 74

Citizen Taxation Request 87

City Charter Election Guidelines, Model 129

The City Council Budget Approval Process 46

City Council Budget Approval Process, The 46

The City Council Finance Committee 45, 46

City Council Finance Committee, The 45, 46

City Manager
     First job 34
     Job interviews xiv, 8, 13, 14, 15, 16, 23, 24, 25,
          26, 27, 30, 63, 73, 74
     Requirements xiv, 25, 30, 35, 40, 47, 48, 52, 59,
          75, 77, 81, 89, 90, 91, 101, 118, 119, 121,
          126, 127, 128, 130, 132, 135, 137

City Manager Job Requirements xiv, 25

City of
     Clifton xi, 6
     Meriden xi, 6
     Oakland xi, 5, 6
     Placentia xi, 6
     Seaside xi, 6
     Vallejo xi, 6

City Politics Change Over Time xv, 99

City Purchasing, Centralized 102

City Resources from Professional Associations and
     Other Organizations, Additional 110

City's Murder Rate, Our 62

City With a Municipal Marina 54

City With a Public Golf Course 55

City With Large Minority Population 33

Closing a Fire Station xiv, 48, 69

Collections, Property Tax 75
Commission, The Chief of Police and the Police 59
Committee, The City Council Finance 45, 46
Complaints, Processing Citizen 81
Conference, A Wonderful Meeting At a 93
Contract Labor Attorney Services 27
Contracts, Union Labor 50

D

Dedication
    Kieran v
Departmental Programs and User Fees 51
Departmental Services Change Over Time xiv, 73
Department Managers, Best Way to Hire 27
Directory, National Resource xv, 128, 139
Directory, State Library 150
Directory, State Municipal League 146
Document, Local Government Historical 125
Doing the Right Thing 23, 28, 30, 39, 63, 78, 83
Doing What Is Right – Getting A City Building
    Permit 91
Downtown Improvements xiv, 106
Downtown, Walking in Our 66, 67

E

Elected Officials xi, xiii, xiv, 1, 2, 8, 9, 11, 12, 13, 14,
    16, 18, 30, 40, 45, 46, 48, 51, 55, 59, 64, 66,
    70, 73, 74, 77, 79, 88, 89, 90, 110, 115, 118,
    123, 159
Election Guidelines, Model City Charter 129
Employee Health Benefits Audit 78
Employee Job Interview Questions 73
Employees, Citizen Complaints About 34

F

Fees, User 8, 51
Final Thoughts, Some 160
Finance and Budgeting Services xiv, 43
Finance Committee, The City Council 45, 46
Fire Fighters and Local Politics xiv, 68
Fire Station, Closing a xiv, 48, 69
Funds for the Homeless Shelter 53
The Future xv, 3, 12, 37, 40, 41, 51, 73, 80, 90, 97,
    100, 105, 108, 120, 123, 144, 156

G

Gifts from Citizens 41
Glossary of Terms 115
Golf Course, City with a Public 55

The Grant Application 17, 18
Guidelines, Model City Charter Election 129
Guidelines, Model County charter Election 134

H

Headquarters of the "Hells Angels" 40, 41
Health Benefits Audit, Employee 78
Hearing Officer, Public xiv, 77
Historical Document, Local Government 125
History, United States Voting Rights 126
Hold Down Property Taxes, Citizen Request to 87
Homeland Security and our Nation's Cities 99
Homeland Security and our State's Cities 101
Homeless, Accommodating the 80
Homeless Shelter, Funds for the 53
How Cities Change Over Time xiii, 3
How Cities Operate and Function xiii, 1
How Mayors Are Elected xiv, 11
How mayors Are Selected 11

I

The Imprisonment Process 82
Imprisonment Process, The 82
Improvements, Downtown xiv, 106
Increases, Police Officer Salary 36
Interview Questions, Employee Job 73
Invited to Speak to Church Leaders 39

J

Job Interview Questions
    Annual Salary 13, 37
    Education xiii, 4, 14, 87, 92, 127, 139, 150
    Employee xiv, 3, 13, 15, 17, 18, 25, 26, 27, 34, 35,
        36, 38, 41, 45, 47, 48, 50, 53, 59, 60, 61,
        65, 69, 70, 73, 74, 76, 77, 78, 79, 81, 83,
        89, 90, 91, 100, 101, 102, 107, 123
Job Opportunities and Desired Locations 6
Job Requirements, City Manager xiv, 25

L

Labor Attorney Services 27
Labor Contracts, Union 50
League Directory, State Municipal 146
Library Director 28, 29
The Library Director 28, 29
Local Government Historical Document 125
Local Politics, Fire Fighters and xiv, 68
Local Politics, Police Officers and 64
Local Restaurant, Police Discounts At a 38

The Location of Polling Places 33
Locations, Regulating Business xiv, 76
Lunch with the Mayor 17

M

Main Street, Trees on Our 79
Maintaining a City's Public Infrastructure xiv, 12
Major University, The Name of a 93
Making Your Shopping Mall Safer 103
Mall Safer, Making Your Shopping 103
Marina, City with a Municipal 54
Mayors
    Request to balance the budget 45
    Letters 15, 16, 20, 78
    Parking tickets 18, 19
    Questions xiv, 13, 14, 15, 16, 23, 27, 39, 40, 46,
        47, 49, 51, 63, 73, 74, 79, 80, 87, 92
    Wanted to see me 19
The Mayor's Letters 15
The Mayor's Parking Tickets 18, 19
The Mayor's Questions 16
Mayor's Request to Balance the Budget 45
Mayor Wanted to See Me 19
Military Base, Police Access to a 36
Minorities 14, 15, 99
Minority Police Officers, More 83
Minority Populations 33, 83
Model City Charter Election Guidelines 129
Model County Charter Election Guidelines 134
More Minority Police Officers 83
Municipal Governments, Names of xiii, 2
Municipal League Directory, State 146
Municipal Marina, City With a 54
Murder Rate, Our City's 62
My Books – Past, Present, and Future 107
My First City Manager Job 24, 33

N

The Name of a Major University 93
Name of a Major University, The 93
Names of Municipal Governments xiii, 2
The Names of Municipal Governments xiii, 2
National Resource Directory xv, 128, 139
Nation's Cities, Homeland Security and Our 99

O

Officer Called, A Police 67
Officer, Public Hearing xiv, 77
Officers, More Minority Police 83

Other City Services xiv, 71
Other City Topics xiv, 85
Our City's Murder Rate 62
Our Downtown, Walking in 66, 67

P

Patrols, Police Walking 66, 107, 109
Personal Property Taxes 52, 89, 90
Police and Fire Services xiv, 51, 57
The Police Commission 59, 60
Police Discounts at a Local Restaurant 38
Police Officer xiv, 33, 36, 37, 38, 39, 40, 41, 45, 60,
    61, 63, 64, 65, 66, 67, 68, 75, 80, 81, 82, 83,
    88, 90, 91, 101, 103, 104, 107, 109
Police Officer Called, A 67
Police Officer Salary Increases 36
Police Officers and Computers 37
Police Officers and Local Politics 64
Police Officers, More Minority 83
Police Officer, Tour of City By 65
Police – Red Light, Being Stopped by the 67
Police, Request from the Chief of 62
Police Services in a Wealthy City 63
Police Walking Patrols 66, 107, 109
Politics Change Over Time, City xv, 99
Politics of City Governments 31
Politics, Police Officers and Local 64
Polling Places, The Location of 33
Population, Minority 33, 83
Possible Budget Reductions xiv, 48
Preface xiii
Privatization of Public Services 90
Processing Citizen Complaints 81
Process, The Chief of Police Appointment 59
Process, The City Council Budget Approval 46
Process, The Imprisonment 82
Professional Department Managers 29, 30
Property Tax Collections xiv, 2, 75, 76
Property Taxes, Personal 52, 89, 90
Property Taxes, Senior Citizens and 88
Property Tax Rate, Compare Your City's 49
Public Golf Course, City With a 55
Public Hearing Officer xiv, 77
Public Infrastructure xiv, 12, 13
Public Property, Citizens Use of 74
Public Services, Privatization of 90
Purchasing, Centralized City 102

Q

Questions, Employee Job Interview 73

R

Rate, Our City's Murder 62
Reductions, Possible Budget xiv, 48
Regulating Business Locations xiv, 76
Request, Citizen Budget 49
Request, Citizen Taxation 87
Request from the Chief of Police 62
Request to Balance the Budget, Mayor's 45
Request to Hold Down Property Taxes, Citizen 87
Resource Directory, National xv, 128, 139
Restaurant, Police Discounts at a Local 38
Right Thing, Doing the 23, 28, 30, 39, 63, 78, 83
Roger L. Kemp, Books by 156
Roger L. Kemp, World Travels by 159

S

Salary Increases, Police Officer 36
Senior Citizens and Property Taxes 88
Services in a Wealthy City, Police 63
The Shopping Mall in Our Towns 104
Shopping Mall Safer, Making Your 103
The Size of Central Park 95
Some Final Thoughts 160
Speaking to Prisoners at the Prison 92
State Library Directory 150
State Municipal League Directory 146
State's Cities, Homeland Security and our 101
Stopped by the Police – Red Light, Being 67

T

Taxation Request, Citizen 87
Tax Collections, Property 75
Taxes, Personal Property 52, 89, 90
Terms, Glossary of 115
Thoughts, Some Final 160
Tour of City by Police Officer 65
Towns, The Shopping Mall in Our 104

U

Union Labor Contracts 50
United States, Immigrants on the West and East
        Coasts of the 105
United States Voting Rights History 126
University of Connecticut, West Hartford, CT 157
Use of Public Property, Citizens 74
User Fees, Departmental Programs and 51

V

Vehicle Taxes, Avoiding 89
Voting Rights History, United States 126

W

Walking in Our Downtown 66, 67
Walking Patrols, Police 66, 107, 109
Ways to Work for An Education 4
Wealthy Community 14, 24, 63
A Wonderful Meeting at a Conference 93
Work Accomplishments 108

Printed in the United States
by Baker & Taylor Publisher Services